Living Life By God's Law

A Study in the Ten Commandments

Gordon Kenworthy Reed

"The light shines in the darkness, and the darkness has not overcome it."
John 1:5

© 2017 Gordon Kenworthy Reed

All rights reserved. No part of this book may be reproduced in any form without written permission from:

Tanglewood Publishing
(800) 241-4016
www.tanglewoodpublishing.org

Cover Image
Moses Receives the Tablets of the Law, 1868
João Zeferino da Costa (1840-1915)

ISBN: 9780997249026
Printed in the United States of America

Book design, layout, and production by Tammy Williams.
E-mail: turtledoveconsult@gmail.com

DEDICATION

This book is dedicated with much affection and
appreciation to all of the faithful followers of
our Lord Jesus Christ who are attempting
to live their lives by God's law.

CONTENTS

Preface ix
Introduction xi
Interpretation and Application 1
God Alone and First 11
Idolatry — A Mental Problem 19
God's Holy Name 27
God's Holy Day 39
Parents — Their Honor and Duty 51
My Brother's Keeper 65
Purity in Heart and Life 73
Dealing with Stealing 85
Speaking and Living the Truth 95
The "Catch-all" Commandment 107
An Old Testament Summary 119
A New Testament Summary 131

PREFACE

I know of no subject more pertinent to the need in America today than that herein treated. As Gordon Reed says, "Across our beloved land ... there is sweeping a dreadful malady that threatens to destroy the foundation ... lawlessness." How does one counter lawlessness?

The Gospel of Jesus Christ counters lawlessness as the law is inscribed afresh in those hearts that are quickened by God's spirit.

> "I will put My law in their minds, and write it on their hearts, and I will be their God and they shall be My people." (Jeremiah 31:33)

But the law prepares the way for the Gospel. And then the Gospel sends us back to the law as God's standard. If the believer is to live a holy life, if he is to bear fruit, he must understand and obey these commandments.

> "He that abides in me and I in him, the same bringeth forth much fruit ... If you keep my commandments you shall abide ..." (John 15:5, 10)

The Christian is to be salt and light in society. In order to perform that function, it is essential that he understand how these commandments speak to our society.

As Gordon Reed points out, many Christians fail to understand the place of the law in the Christian life. I think of one noted Christian educator who wrote, "God never speaks to believers in tones of law," and "For the Christian the law is a dead and useless thing." How tragic! Rather in the words of Calvin, "... as we need not only instruction but also exhortation, the servant of God will derive this further advantage from the law; by frequent meditation on it he will be excited to obedience, he will be confirmed in it, and restrained from the slippery path of transgression."[1] Wesley said: "The third use of the law is to keep us alive. It is the grand means whereby the blessed Spirit prepares the believer for larger communication of the life of God."[2] Do you want such larger communications? I do.

A word about our author. It has been my privilege to know Gordon Reed as a fellow pastor for fifteen years. He represents to me what a pastor should be. As the reader will find, he is a very effective and faithful expositor of God's Word. Not only is he an excellent communicator, a warm pastor, and excellent administrator, but he is a leader in Christ's Church. I deeply appreciate his willingness to stand for truth whenever and wherever duty has called. With more men like this, God willing, the tide could be turned.

> Frank M. Barker, Jr.
> Pastor Emeritus
> Briarwood Presbyterian Church
> Birmingham, Alabama

---

[1] Calvin, *Institutes of the Christian Religion,* II, vii-12
[2] Wesley, *Christian Theology,* ed. Thornley Smith, p. 175

INTRODUCTION

The purpose of this book is to give a short, concise, and easily read guide to understanding the Ten Commandments. It is my hope that this short book will enable the reader to discover the intention of God in each commandment, and the application of these laws to our lives in today's world. It is not written in the language of the theologian, nor the linguistic scholar. There is a place, of course, for such works, but the intention of the author differs from this. This study is written by a working pastor whose purpose is to explain the meaning of God's Word to busy people who need help in understanding and applying God's Word to their lives. For this reason, the scholar will find little help and nothing new in this book. That is fine. He has other sources for his search. However, the Sunday school teacher, the home Bible study leader, and perhaps even the busy and often harried pastor who must prepare and present several messages every week, may all find it helpful in their efforts. They may even find it more helpful than other works of more scholarly dimension.

When one views the Christian scene today, there is much division and confusion. Old denominational boundary lines are not nearly so significant as other matters which divide the Church. There is of course one great dividing line in the Christian world today, and that has to do with the view of Scripture. This line crosses many others, and is the real crux of all controversy in the Church. Is the Bible the word of

God in the full and infallible sense of the word, or is it something less? Is it God's self-disclosure given by immediate revelation through chosen vessels, or is it the best of man's ideas of God which he has learned over the centuries of his existence? These two positions are poles apart, and may not be reconciled save by serious compromise or total capitulation by one side or the other.

Within the camp of those who seriously believe the Bible is the Word of God — the only infallible, inerrant rule of faith and life — there are many, many divisions and disagreements. Nowhere is this seen more clearly than the varying positions on the whole matter of the place of God's law in the life of the believer.

There are some who claim to be nothing more than "New Testament Christians." By this term, they intend to say that the Old Testament is relatively unimportant. Some go farther than this. Several years ago, a leading sports figure who had been widely hailed and loudly lauded for his conversion to Christianity wrote a letter to one of the more widely read Christian periodicals protesting an article which had rather mildly suggested that professional sports on the Lord's Day were inappropriate. This man was livid with self-righteous rage. (He of course made a fabulous salary by playing football on Sunday.) He emphatically shouted that Christians were free from any obligation to the Old Testament law. His words were blasphemous. One can only hope his ignorance excused him (though it seldom does). "To hell with the Ten Commandments," he wrote. "Christ has set me free from the law." Admittedly, that is an extreme position and shockingly so, but mind you, this man was in heavy demand as a speaker for many churches, youth camps, evangelistic crusades and the like. This would suggest that such views are tolerated by many, and in fact, to a lesser extent, are the views of many Christians towards the law. This is very sad and very dangerous. It makes me exceedingly nervous to live on the same block with the man who says, "I am free from the Ten Commandments." Does this mean he is free to steal from me, to bear false witness against me, to covet my possessions, and if all else fails, to kill me?

Let's look at the other side of the coin: the ugly beast of legalism raises its head in each generation. There are several forms of this. There is the old, though still widely held, form of legalism which majors in the minors. This is an offspring of a very narrow fundamentalism which quickly condemns all Christians who disagree with anything such as man or Church might hold, whether biblically based or not. This type of legalism tends to identify a Christian as one who does not engage in certain "questionable" activities such as drinking, smoking, attending movies, etc. Now it is true that the conscientious believer will think about such things to see if they are a stumbling block to himself or others. Many will come to the conclusion that such activities have no place in their life. But that is quite a different thing than the legalist's position.

This problem is not new. It is as old as the Church itself. The Galatian heresy with which the apostle Paul had to deal in no uncertain terms was a form of legalism which simply refused to go away in spite of the Jerusalem Council and in spite of all Paul wrote and preached. This heresy taught that though we are saved by grace, yet we must also continue in the things of the Old Testament to be in a state of grace and a right relationship with God. It had even reached the point of teaching, "no circumcision, no salvation." Those who held such views were known as the Judaizers. These were people who confessed Christ and were a part of the Church, but for zeal's sake insisted that circumcision was an absolute necessity for salvation. Paul's rebuke may seem severe, but the Gospel was at stake. "If you insist on circumcision, Christ profits you nothing!" In his decisive letter to the Galatians, which may have been the turning point in this controversy, he recalls that it was even necessary to rebuke Peter to his face in public assembly because he, too, was carried away in his conduct by these Judaizers.[1]

There is a rebirth of that heresy today in the form of an extreme theonomy position.[2] It is not confined to any one denomination, though it seems that several branches of churches holding a Reformed persuasion have more than their share of theonomists in their midst. It is difficult to see exactly where the theonomists cross the line between a commendable zeal for God's law, and a heretical stance of denying pivotal and non-negotiable truth, but there is such a line and it has obviously been transgressed many times. One hallmark of those who hold this position is fanatical anger against those who oppose their position. Paul knew their wrath in Galatia, and those who speak out against this dangerous teaching in our time catch the brunt of their wrath. While it is not the intention of this book to engage in toe to toe debate, and point for point confrontation with these modern day Judaizers, it is hoped that this work will present the reader with a positive and biblically consistent exposition of the place of God's law in the life of believers. In this way, the error of the theonomists will be refuted without excessive polemics which tend to divide rather than instruct.

The real battle over the place of God's law is not being waged within the cloistered walls of academic pursuit, but in the courts and Congress of our nation. God's law is under assault by the secularists who are determined to rid themselves and all mankind from the shackles of moral law of any sort. Their position is clear: there is no set standard of right and wrong for all men and nations. They reject the existence of God and, therefore, His moral law. It becomes the believer's responsibility before God to demonstrate through his or her life an obedience to God's law, and to work for a society in which the basic principles of the Ten Commandments become the underlying foundation for all laws — which seek to establish justice and order in the lives of those who bind themselves together in a body politic. It is my hope and sincere prayer that the Lord might use the message of this book to help believers accomplish both these ends in their lives.

ENDNOTES

[1] Book of Galatians. (It is suggested that a good commentary on Galatians be obtained for a more detailed summary of these problems.)

[2] For a brief but excellent paper on theonomy, see *Theonomy: An Assessment Its Implications for Church and Society*. Paul B. Fowler, Reformed Theological Seminary, Jackson, Mississippi.

FOR FURTHER STUDY

1. *Commentary on Galatians*: Herman N. Ridderbos Th.D. (New International Commentary on New Testament)
2. *Commentary on Galatians*: Martin Luther
3. *Theonomy Examined*: Paul B. Fowler, Reformed Theological Seminary
4. *Theonomy: An Assessment*: Paul B. Fowler, Reformed Theological Seminary

Chapter 1

INTERPRETATION AND APPLICATION

"The law of the Lord is perfect, converting the soul."[1] Across our beloved land today, and indeed across the whole world, there is sweeping a dreadful malady that threatens to destroy the foundation and the whole structure of our way of life. This disease is far more deadly than the black plague which virtually depopulated much of western Europe in the early Middle Ages. It is a greater threat than the world-wide communist conspiracy which has devoured much of the world.

This malady has many names and even more explanations. It is being ignored by some, excused by others, but it gathers momentum every day. It infects young and old, rich and poor, male and female. By whatever name it is called, it is basically one thing: lawlessness. It will, if unchecked, destroy us. From a human perspective, there seems little chance of stopping its deadly march. It has reached the point that many, even some in high places, seem to think that those who oppose this lawlessness and defend us against its inroads are the real villains, and the law breakers are the heroes, or at least the innocent victims. Woe unto us, we are a nation ripe for judgment.

In our confusion, fright, and moral chaos, where can we turn? To whom may we go? At one time, the government was the refuge from this plague. But now government seems confused and at times unable and unwilling to protect its citizenry against lawlessness. Surely the Church will take its stand, or will it? Far too often, the Church leaders are in the forefront of those protesting law enforcement and defending law breakers. Even when this is not true, many times the Church simply turns within itself and hides behind the cliché, "the separation of church and state." There is still a rock of defense against this foe. Even today amidst the chaotic moral state of our nation and world, the crumbling institutions and ideals of yesteryear, there is an ancient code which embodies all truths upon which law and order stand. This ancient code is known by all men, indeed to an extent it is written into their hearts. It was engraven upon tablets of stone, signifying its unchanging character and timeless truth. I refer, of course, to God's moral law: the Ten Commandments.

The people of Israel had wandered for long weeks and months in the desert wilderness of Sinai. For many centuries, they and their fathers before them had been the slave class of the great Egyptian civilization. Four hundred years of bitter bondage had come to an abrupt and dramatic end when Jehovah God had raised up Moses to deliver his covenant people from Pharoah's cruel thralldom. Through the fury of ten plagues, the might of Egypt and even the iron will of the tyrant had been broken, and Israel was free. They had been delivered by the mighty hand of the God of Abraham, Isaac, and Jacob, who heard their cry for salvation. In the process, they had been spared when the angel of death brought the tenth and last plague upon the stubborn Pharoah. By the word of God, the blood of God's lamb was sprinkled over the doorposts of Israel's homes and the angel of death passed over them, but destroyed all the firstborn of Egypt, both man and beast, high and low.

They were brought out of Egypt. The waters of the Red Sea were parted to allow them to pass, but overwhelmed the pursuing Egyptians to their doom. Alone in the wilderness and threatened with starvation and thirst, God fed them manna from heaven and brought out water from the rocks. He defended them from fierce desert foes, and sent a cloud by day and a pillar of fire by night to lead them. Now they had come to the mount of God where they would remain for the better part of a year. Here they would receive food and water for their souls. Here they would be given more sure guidance than a cloud and fire. Here they would find refuge from the most implacable foe. For from the holy mount, God would reveal to them His own character and His law. They were the people of God by grace and salvation; now they would become the people of God by covenant and obedience. It was time for them to learn the meaning of salvation in terms of obedience to the will and word of the Savior God.

This was one of the most important and dramatic days

in the history of the world — the day God's law was engraven on tablets of stone. These ten commandments would serve forever as a revelation of God's own character and His will for redeemed people. This law became the solid rock upon which the nation of Israel was founded. It has served ever since as the standard by which all law must be judged.

Millennia have passed and there are those who think the law is out of date, passé, no longer applicable to modern man. Perfectly sincere (but sadly wrong) people will tell you that the Christian is free from the law. The Ten Commandments will never be out of date. God's covenant people will never be "free" from the revelation of God's righteousness. Of course, Christ has freed us from the curse of the law, having borne the curse for us. We are truly under grace, and thank God for it. Still, these same commandments form the basis for Godly living for those who are free from its curse. Here is the pathway of a life well-pleasing to God and honoring His son. Jesus said, "Think not that I have come to destroy the law and prophets: I have not come to destroy, but to fulfill."[2] He went on to say, "Whosoever breaks one of the least of these commandments, and teaches men to do likewise, the same shall be called the least in the kingdom of Heaven."[3]

The importance of the Ten Commandments may be best understood by considering the one who gave them. If the law of God is out of date, then God must be out of date as well. This law was given in the most direct God-man encounter in history. When God revealed the law, He revealed Himself. He revealed that He was God alone, saying, "I am the Lord." Why is there an absolute standard of right and wrong? Because there is a sovereign God who created the world and who has a purpose and plan for that creation. No God, no law. That is why the law of God is being ignored and rejected today. People have rejected the God of the Bible as being unreal or unworthy of their devotion. The autonomy of man has become the religion of the culture and of the state. We are beginning to realize how dangerous and destructive this philosophy is, and how dangerous are the people who follow it. In the very name by which God revealed Himself to Moses, first at the burning bush in the wilderness and now from the mountain of fire, He reveals His nature and character. He is Jehovah, the eternal God of time and eternity, before whom all nations are as a drop in the bucket or a speck of dust upon the scales.

But God also reveals Himself as a personal and saving God, saying, "I am the Lord, thy God, who has brought thee out of the land of Egypt, out from the house of bondage."[4] He is Lord of nations and history, and He is also the God of the individual. Christians are a part of a covenant people, just as Israel of old, but it is also necessary to have that personal relationship with Him. God has always spoken to man as the Savior God. Even in the garden, when man was confronted with consequences of his sin and rebellion, he was sought out by God and provision was made for his covering and care.

The message of grace begins in Genesis 3:15 and continues down through biblical history as the unifying theme of all Scripture. When the world of Noah passed the point of no return, and when judgment became inevitable, still Noah found grace in the eyes of the Lord and inherited the rainbow after the deluge.

It is well and necessary to remember that the God who says to you, "you shall" and "you shall not" is the God who says, "I am the Lord thy God who has brought you out of the land of Egypt, out of the house of bondage." This saving and loving God issues His law from a heart of love as well as holiness. He knows that only those who live in harmony with His law will know the delights of a close walk with Him, and the full joy of their salvation.

It is important at this point to further consider to whom this law was given. It was never given to any people as a means of their salvation — never, never, never. Rather, God gave redeemed people the law as a guide for redeemed living. Israel was not a perfect people, but they were a redeemed nation, in debt to mercy and called to reveal the glories of Him who had saved them. The Christian is in much the same situation. We are saved unto good works that we might show forth the glories of Him who called us from darkness into His marvelous light. This is a very important thing to keep in mind. We are upset and rightly so at the lawlessness that plagues our land. However, Christian people must bear their part of the blame for this deplorable situation. How may we expect the unlearned and unsaved to honor God's law when we openly ignore it? We are shocked at the blatant attempt to remove any vestige of a holy day from the affairs of our nation, but Christians, too, join in the breaking of God's law by pretending His law concerning the Sabbath simply does not exist. We buy, sell, work, and play on the Lord's Day as on any other day all the while protesting, "but I went to church this morning." We are distressed at the idolatry of humanism, but have we not put idols of success and pleasure before God? This generation of Christians needs to take seriously the warning of Scripture, "judgment must begin at the house of God."[5] If only those who openly identify with the cause of Christ will demonstrate an obedience to God's law, we would see a dramatic recovery of ideals and integrity in our country.

At this point, allow me to remind you of the purpose, or purposes, of the law. For believers, it serves two primary functions: preparation for the Gospel, and instruction in righteousness. The first step in receiving Christ as personal Savior from sin is an acute awareness of sin. The law shows us what God expects, and at the same time convinces us how utterly impossible it is for us to meet this expectation. The law is holy and good, but we are not. The law of the Lord is perfect, and it tells us of our imperfections. In short, it brings conviction of sin. We hear the Lord Jesus say, "Be ye therefore perfect even as your Father in heaven is perfect,"[6] and by these words we stand condemned by the law's revelation of that holy perfection. In the words of Paul, "The law is our truant officer to bring us to Christ."[7] Having been convicted by the law, and made to appear guilty before God, our only hope is in the mercy revealed at the cross. There, the only Man in history to ever perfectly keep the holy law was condemned and killed as if He were a lawbreaker. There, God the Son in the person of Jesus of Nazareth offered Himself up to God the Father in our behalf that all the requirements of the law might be met for us, including its penalty of death.

Even as the law was given to show Israel how to live in the way of righteousness, we who have been driven to the cross by the law's demands now become those who delight in the law of God in the inner man. We want to please Him who saved us. We want to demonstrate that the New Covenant promise has been realized in us … that God would write His law on our hearts. By His law, we judge and correct our behavior. It becomes His plumb line for our daily lives; His straight-edge for our conduct. We see no contradiction between law and grace, but a harmony of the two.

Finally, let me point out some broader implications of the law. These ten words are more than just specific commandments. They are foundational principles for all laws. They are comprehensive, covering all relationships between God and man, and between men. They are foundation stones upon which all civilization rests. They form the basis for civil law and for Church law. Remove the foundation and the structure built upon it will crumble in short time. This is why the rejection of this code of laws by modern man is so tragic. Little does he understand that human freedom depends upon acceptance and enforcement of these laws. While he struggles to free himself from what he imagines are the shackles of these laws, he brings upon himself bondage and enslavement. The political, economic, social, and religious enslavement of communism and other forms of totalitarian government will eventually cover the whole earth unless there is a return to these laws as the only sure foundation for our freedom. The hour is late but the task is not impossible. It is for the Church to set the example and lead the crusade back from the brink of the abyss. If we succeed, future generations will arise and call us blessed. If we fail, the new "dark ages" are upon us. The enemy is not only at the gate; he is within the walls. We must awaken now, or we shall surely perish.

ENDNOTES

[1] Psalm 19:7
[2] Matthew 5:17
[3] Matthew 5:19
[4] Exodus 20:2
[5] 1 Peter 4:17
[6] Matthew 5:48
[7] Galatians 3:24

FOR FURTHER STUDY

1. Westminster Larger Catechism Questions and Answers 91-101
2. *A Christian Manifesto* by Francis Schaeffer
3. Does the law reveal only the holiness and justice of God?
4. What other attributes of God does it reveal?
5. In what sense is the law of God applicable to non-Christians?
6. In what sense is the Christian "free" from the law?
7. How is obedience to God's law a fulfillment of the New Testament command, "Be filled with the Spirit"?

Chapter 2

GOD ALONE AND FIRST

"I am the Lord thy God who brought thee out of the land of Egypt, out of the house of bondage. Thou shalt have no other gods before Me."[1] "Thou shalt love the Lord thy God with all thy heart, and with all thy soul, and with all thy mind, and with all thy strength. This is the first and great commandment."[2]

By these words from God through His servant Moses and through His Son the Lord Jesus, we learn of the first commandment. This commandment is not only first in order, but also first in importance both to God and for us. It describes the first duty of man to God and the foundation for all other laws. It is the basis for our relationship with God, and in a very real sense all our relationships with other people. If this law is taken seriously and if we truly obey its requirements, all other laws will fall in place and we will delight in the inner man after the law of God. But if this commandment is ignored, then we will pay little heed to any law which God might give to us.

This law speaks to the deep need of man to know God and to know His will. Do you know why you find it so difficult or even impossible to keep the third commandment, the seventh, or the tenth? Because the first is broken. Here is the foundation, the cornerstone, and key for obedience to all that God requires. When this law is ignored, it becomes impossible to obey any others. God commands that He be given first place, that He alone be adored and worshipped as God, and that none supplant Him in your life. Most, if not all of us, give mental assent to this law, but it does not always appear that this assent is carried over into actual practice. In fact, when we honestly begin to assess our priorities, we discover that all too often we give first place to many other things. This law applies to worship, but not only to worship. It requires that in all things God be given first place. Do your priorities teach your children that God has first place in your family? What percentage of your time is spent in family worship as compared to family TV time? Have we structured God out of His rightful place? ("I really would like to make God first place in my life if I ever had the time.")

One of the most difficult things in life is to bring our practice into harmony with our creed. I read recently the results of a Gallup poll taken to determine the percentage of people in America who believe in a personal God. It was astounding! 87% of those polled professed to believe; yet, one is forced to ask the question: Do 87% of the American people live as if there is a personal God? Few people are atheistic in their theoretical position, but many are practicing atheists, living as if there is no God.

This brings us to the first and most obvious thing this

law forbids. It forbids atheism in any form. Communism is based on the premise that there is no God save man himself, and promises a glorious future for the human race as a result of the practice of social, political, and economic communism. Secular humanism, the grandson of deism, which has become almost the official state religion of the United States, teaches basically the same thing. This philosophy rejects God and any set standard of right and wrong. Since this philosophy has prevailed in the courts and in the educational system of our land, prayer has been outlawed in public schools, Bible reading has been forbidden, and the Ten Commandments have been taken down from the walls of the classroom. Like communism, this philosophy promised a bright future based on man's freedom from God, but like communism, it enslaves the mind, and turns wise men into fools.

As dangerous as these forms of atheism are — and they are deadly — the Christian has more to fear from practical atheism, which is so insidious and equally enslaving. It is so easy to fall into its trap. It is so easy to live as if there is no God, or that He is not really important, or as if the living God is no more than an idol of wood or metal … deaf, dumb, and blind. Any time we live as if God is no more than Santa Claus or a kindly old grandfather (I have nothing against kindly old grandfathers; in fact I am one) we are breaking this commandment.

This commandment also forbids and condemns idolatry in any form. Pride makes a god of self. Lust makes a god of passion, covetousness makes a god of material things. Which of these rule in your life? Before which throne do you bow down?

This commandment forbids a host of other sins. 1) This law forbids unbelief. When the devil tempted Jesus in the wilderness, "Command these stones that they become bread,"[3] he was tempting Him to doubt the Father's power to provide for His needs. In short, it was the temptation of unbelief. Jesus rebuked the devil and passed the test. We are not always that successful. 2) It also forbids that we tempt the Lord. Cast yourself down from the pinnacle of the temple, God will bear you up. Place yourself in places and positions of great temptation, God will deliver you. So Satan tempted Jesus, so he tempts people today. 3) It forbids needless anxiety and worry. 4) It forbids prayerlessness and insincere worship of God. 5) It forbids the cold formalism of worship that has no awe or reverence of God. I would strongly suggest you read and study most carefully what the Westminster Larger Catechism has to say about this commandment, and also the supporting scriptures to which it points.

There is a positive side to this law. It teaches us who God is and to love the Lord with all our hearts. It tells us to put God first in life. What is first in yours? Jesus said,

"Seek the kingdom of God and all these things will be added unto you." NO! That's not what He said. He said: "Seek first the kingdom of God and His righteousness and all these things will be added unto you."[4] Unless God comes first in our seeking, we cannot claim the promises of added blessings. God refuses to take second place. He just won't be next in line in your life. God will either be God in your life or He will be out of your life. So this law teaches us to put God first. It teaches us to love God with all our heart; love Him enough to know Him, His will, and His law. I was telling a group of seminarians what they might expect in the ministry. I told them they could expect to live on the ragged edge of total physical, mental, and emotional exhaustion all the time, and that still would not be enough. In a sense, every Christian faces this requirement. After we have done all we can do, still we must bow before the living God and say, "I am an unworthy and unprofitable servant."

Loving Him means more than just an inward affection and delight in Him. Loving Him also means to love those whom He loves and to love what He loves. Who and what does God love? He loves His Son, for He said of the Lord Jesus, "This is my beloved Son, in whom I am well pleased." To obey the first commandment, we must love God's Son and trust Him as Savior. There are sects and cults all around us who, though professing to love God and His Son, refuse to honor the Lord Jesus with the position Scripture accords

Him. They do not honor Him as God the Son. We must utterly reject such groups and not encourage them in any way by accepting their literature or allowing them in our homes, except to hear our witness to the Lord Jesus. God loves His Son's bride, the Church. Can you imagine someone telling you they love your son, but hate his wife? That would be an insult and an absurdity. You would reject such a person. How do you think God feels towards those who hold the Church in contempt, and who yet profess to love His Son? A good and true test of your love for God is your attitude towards the Church. Do you love the Church?

The Bible teaches that God loves mercy, truth, purity, kindness, humility, and a cheerful giver. To put God first is to love by practicing these virtues.

To love God is also to hate the things He hates. "God hates a proud look and lying tongue, hands that shed innocent blood, a heart that devises wicked imaginations, feet that are swift in running to mischief, a false witness, and he that sows discord among brethren."[5] He hates hypocrisy, injustice, cruelty, and oppression of the poor and weak. These things God hates, and those who love Him must hate them, too, especially when they appear in their own hearts and lives.

Above all, this law requires that my eager love for the Lord should express itself in obedience to all He commands. Jesus said, "If you love, me keep my commandments."

How may I prove my love for the Lord, that He truly has first place in my life? By simple obedience to what He requires of me.

The Westminster Larger Catechism rightly calls attention to certain words in this commandment which are overlooked: the words "before me."[7] It raises the question, why are these words included, and goes on to answer this question by saying: "These words 'before me' in the first commandment teach us that God who sees all things takes notice of, and is much displeased with, the sin of having any other God." Very simply, this means that the most important thing about this commandment is that we practice obedience to it before God. We must answer to Him both in this life and in the life to come. "For we must all appear before the judgment seat of Christ to give an account of the things done in the body whether good or bad."[8]

ENDNOTES

[1] Exodus 20:2 [2] Matthew 22:37, 38 [3] Luke 4:3
[4] Matthew 6:33 [5] Proverbs 6:16-19 [6] John 14:15
[7] Westminster Larger Catechism Question and Answer 106
[8] II Corinthians 5:11

FOR FURTHER STUDY

1. Westminster Larger Catechism Questions and Answers 103-106.
2. Is it possible for a Christian to break this law?
3. What are some gods of modern man?
4. Why is atheism a violation of this law?
5. What are some ways "secular humanism" and Communism are in agreement?
6. How does one "seek first the kingdom of God and His righteousness"?

Chapter 3

IDOLATRY — A MENTAL PROBLEM

"Thou shalt not make unto thee any graven image ... thou shalt not bow down thyself to them ..."[1] The first commandment tells us that God is to be loved and worshipped. The second tells us how, and how not, to express this worship and love. The two commandments are not one as some suppose, but are closely related. The God who requires us to love Him with all our hearts and worship Him alone, also reveals to us how this love and worship are to be expressed. It is the duty of believers to search the scriptures to discover the proper way to worship God, and to give Him that worship He requires of us with pure and sincere hearts.

The Westminster Larger Catechism, in dealing with the duties taught by this commandment, goes into considerable detail to show just what manner of worship the word of God commands. It is consistent with the spirit and commitment of the Westminster divines that nothing is proposed that does not pass the test of direct spiritual warrant.

It might be well to note that in the history of the Church there is a pattern which occurs with distressing frequency. When great emphasis is placed on forms of worship, especially ones that emphasize Church tradition over biblical warrant, there is usually a parallel decline in doctrine and holy living according to God's Word. It is almost as if some think God can be appeased by forms, rather than worshipped in spirit and in truth.

    Since this commandment is expressed in negative language, let us first see what it forbids and something of the nature of idolatry. The major sin forbidden by this law is the sin of idolatry. We are not to think of God in the form of some visual image we may make of Him. The genesis of idolatry is in the mind of man, fallen man. The idolator does not set out to create a new God, but simply to represent the God he worships in some visual way expressly intended to convey the nature of that God. Men of old sought out skilled craftsmen who were instructed by priests, or perhaps the priests themselves became skilled craftsmen for purposes of monetary gain. Such craftsmen took precious metals, gold or silver, and fashioned a visual representation of a god; before this idol men fell down and worshipped. In time, the image itself became not a means of worship, but an object of worship. Though it was nothing more than a skillfully constructed form of metal, yet men ascribed to it great power. They prayed to it as if it had ears that could actually hear. They sought its help as if its still, cold arms actually had great and saving power. They sought from it guidance as if it had eyes that could really see. The image was venerated, adored, and worshipped. Because the mind that conceived it was a fallen mind, and the hand that fashioned it was of a fallen mind, the idol was ordinarily grotesque, absurd, and often obscene. It generated great fear and dread in the minds of those who came before it.

If a man was so poor he could not afford an idol of precious metal, he might chop down a tree and carve an image from its stump, and fall down before such an image and entreat its mercy and help. He would never stop to think that he had used part of the same wood to build a house or a fire.[2]

Israel was surrounded by people who worshipped after this fashion, and history records that in spite of this explicit commandment, she often fell into similar habits. One of the major themes of the Old Testament is the folly and sin of breaking the second commandment. The prophets found themselves locked in deadly combat with prophets of Baal and other gods. By the word of God, they roundly condemned the accompanying practices of idolatry such as human sacrifice and sexual immorality as an expression of worship. A little better understanding of the gods and goddesses of fertility and all that was involved in their worship enables one to see why God continually refers to idolatry as "whoredom." It was just that in every sense of the word.

We are living in another age. Does that mean the sin of idolatry is no longer a major threat? Not at all, for many people in the world still worship graven images, idols of gold, silver, stone, and wood. Many Christian people ignore this prohibition and worship — or attempt to worship — God through images, statues, pictures ... man-made forms of worship and ritual. They protest these things are simply aids to worship but, by so doing, they refute God's authority to command the fact and nature of true worship which he requires. Let's go one step further and admit it might be possible for people who abhor such things to be blind to their own expressions of making graven images. We might identify God so closely with some man-made formulation of doctrine that we would end up worshipping those words and forms rather than the God of Scripture. We might protest that these things are only aids to worship, but that has a familiar ring to it, doesn't it? We must be very careful while attempting to remove the speck from our brother's eye that we do not overlook the log in our own. If we are tempted to explain our religious customs on the basis of "reformed tradition," we would do well to study again the Larger Catechism on this commandment.

This is one of the commandments with reasons attached to it, and we do well to consider God's reasoning. Any time God gives reasons for His requirement, we should listen to those reasons. The reasons for this law are stated in a declaration, a warning, and a promise. The declaration is that God is a jealous God. This means that God will not share His glory with another. He will not be thought of according to man's reasoning, but only according to His own self-revelation. It is insulting to the majesty and glory of God to make a graven image of Him according to man's imagination. It is just as insulting to God to reject biblical revelation about Him at any point by saying, "But I just can't believe in a God who ..." Usually, such a statement is protesting some biblical truth about God, such as His righteousness, wrath, or absolute sovereignty. God is a jealous God in that He would not have man drawn astray and destroyed by his own evil imagination. The declaration is followed by a warning: "Visiting the iniquities of the fathers upon the children unto the third and fourth generations of them that hate me."[3] Idolatry is a form of God-hatred, not God worship. Idolatry is hating God because it is rejecting the true God for a God of our own desire and imagination. The warning of wrath should be taken seriously. What happens when men insist on their own ideas of God over biblical revelation? Their children follow them in that sin. Even as a man tends to become like the god he worships for good or ill, so a child tends to become like his parents. Once again, the history of the Church shows that once steps are taken in the wrong direction, they leave a long trail that many generations will follow. This is why it is so important that our worship be always according to God's Word and constantly reformed and brought back to biblical patterns.

    The final words of these reasons are in the form of a promise: "... showing mercy unto thousands [of generations] of them that love me and keep my commandments."[4] Just as idolatry is a form of God-hatred, so true worship is an expression of God-love. Those who seek the Lord will find Him. Those who seek Him in His revelation honor Him with the seeking and the finding. Those who worship Him in spirit and in truth are sought by God. They find blessing and reward for themselves, for God is the rewarder of those who seek Him. They also bring the blessing of God upon their offspring throughout the passing generations. His loving kindness extends to thousands compared to His wrath that extends to the fourth generation. The contrast is intentional. Are we not the living proof of this promise? Our forefathers sought out a land where they might worship God according to His word (not "as they pleased," as some versions have it). They paid the price for the freedom to teach their children the Word and the proper worship of God. God honored their efforts. We today who follow in their train inherit the blessings they won for us. Let us make very sure we secure the same blessing for our offspring.

ENDNOTES

[1] Exodus 20:4-5
[2] The two paragraphs above are paraphrases of Isaiah 44:9-20.
[3] Exodus 20:5
[4] Exodus 20:6

FOR FURTHER STUDY

1. Westminster Larger Catechism Questions and Answers 107-110.
2. Why is idolatry a "mental problem"?
3. What is your definition of an idol?
4. Why is it dangerous to attempt to represent God by some symbol or picture?
5. Does this command forbid all religious art? Why or why not?

Chapter 4

GOD'S HOLY NAME

"Thou shalt not take the name of the Lord thy God in vain, for the Lord will not hold him guiltless who taketh His name in vain."[1] "O Lord, our Lord, how excellent is thy name in all the earth."[2] When Jesus taught His disciples to pray, He said: "In this manner pray: Our Father who art in heaven, hallowed be thy name."[3] When defending the cause of Christ before the Sanhedrin, Simon Peter, who shortly before had said of the Lord Jesus, "I do not know Him," now boldly declares of the same Jesus, "There is no other name under heaven given among men, whereby we must be saved."[4]

The Word of God clearly teaches that the name of God is to be held in honor and used only in reverence by those who speak it.

When I was a teenager (many years ago) one of the fads we enjoyed was "What's in a name?" The idea was to discover the origin and meaning of your name. Everyone seemed to think it was a lot of fun and often hilarious, especially when names and people were evidently mismatched. But when you think about it, your name is very important. It may well be your greatest asset, and it could be your greatest liability, depending on how you have treated that name by your conduct. Your name tells other people who you are.

It links you with the past and the future. Your name tells what kind of person you are. Your name and reputation are inseparably woven together. Sometimes, we may be helped or hindered by our names which we share in common with others. Several years ago, when I was involved in the beginning days of Ridge Haven, the conference center for the Presbyterian Church in America, a retired family from south Florida moved into the community. They were unpleasantly surprised to discover that they were unable to cash a check, to obtain credit, or even to be socially accepted by the people. The problem was their name, which they bore in common with certain families in a nearby village who had a bad reputation. It took a while to convince people they were of no kin, nor did they share in the bad habits and misconduct of the other families with the same last name.

There are certain names stored in your memory vault, and from time to time you take them out and look at them and remember. Maybe you shed a tear, or a deep sigh, a laugh, or at least a smile. For some of those names, you thank the Lord for all that those persons meant and still mean to you. There are some names you wish you could forget.

We are living in a time when literally billions of dollars are spent annually just to make you aware of certain names, and then to keep those names constantly before you. These are called brand names, and the idea is to make you associate that certain name with a particular product, whether it is a refrigerator, or an automobile, or just toothpaste. This idea has been applied to our political campaigns. Just think of the millions which have been spent to keep the names of office-seekers in your mind. Most campaigns for public office are won or lost because of the familiarity of the name and the associations that are made with that name. The candidates' efforts are directed towards making you have positive reactions when you hear his or her name. In some situations, a name may get you a job or get you fired. It may help you get credit, or assure that you will never have credit.

God puts tremendous importance on His name. He knows that His name and character are tied together. The name of God tells us who He is and what He has done for our salvation. Therefore, He has placed the requirement of reverence for His name in the Ten Commandments, which are the basic guiding principles upon which all laws of Church and state rest. These ten words provide the framework for all true religion and all human relationships. This commandment takes its place of equal importance with such laws as "Thou shall not kill." In many other places throughout all Scripture, the importance of God's name is strongly emphasized.

When the Lord Jesus was praying to the Father in the presence of His disciples the prayer we commonly call the high priestly prayer, He made this statement: "I have glorified thee on earth, having accomplished the work which thou hast given me to do." Then He went on to describe that work in these words: "I manifested thy name to the men whom thou gavest me out of the world."[5] He understood His whole mission on earth was to reveal the name, and thus the character, of God to those whom God had chosen to be His own from before the foundation of the earth. That would involve the cross and the resurrection, for apart from these, neither the justice nor the mercy of God would ever be understood.

The names by which God reveals Himself in the Bible reveal to us the kind of God we know and worship. They speak of His eternity, His omnipotence, His sovereignty. They also tell us the relationship He has with us as a covenant-making and covenant-keeping God. A very beneficial study for any believer would be a careful and thorough investigation of all the titles, names, and attributes by which God reveals Himself to man.

To start on a human level, when you think of the name "Jesus," what does that bring to mind? Savior, shepherd, the cross, salvation. When you think of the name Father, you think of one who loves his children, one who provides for them, one who delights to give his children good things. When you think of the Holy Spirit, you think of comfort, guidance, enlightenment, conviction. You may wish to go beyond this and make a careful linguistic study of the various names and titles of God to further enrich your understanding of Him. You will also discover that your love and reverence for Him will grow as well.

Can there be any doubt that one of the great crying needs of this present generation is to recapture a sense of reverence for God's name? Can there be any doubt that one of the greatest sins of modern man is the breaking of this holy law? When one considers the warning, "For the Lord will not hold him guiltless who takes His name in vain,"[6] one can but tremble for this generation. It is sad to say, but obviously true, that even many Christians fall into this sin. Ours is a careless and profane age. The name of God is held in open contempt in many quarters. Isn't it terribly sad to think that many children growing up today learn from their parents and others that God's name is only to be used when you want to curse or swear, when you're angry or hurt, when you're surprised or when you're amazed? We must contest that use. We must rebuke that terrible abuse. Today's child hears this from every quarter: from parents, from other children, from television programs (which even Christian parents fail to censor), from teachers and coaches, from prominent politicians, from the sports idol whom he has come to worship. But God's ancient law remains unchanged and His warning is still in force. Many people mock at what they consider to be old ideas, but the Bible says, "Fools make mock at sin."[7] Reverence for God's name is a must. If we are to obey this command, and refrain from violating God's holy name, we must make sure we thoroughly understand all that it teaches and all it forbids.

Obviously, it condemns and forbids certain sins, and the most obvious of all is the sin of profanity. The Bible makes very clear that is one of the most destructive of all sins. Destructive of your relationship with God as well as your integrity is the sin of the careless lip and the profane tongue. Very often, a person will use God's name in vain and then protest, "Oh that just slipped out." That's really not true. The words we speak reveal the inner attitude and condition of the heart. Truly, you are what you say. The wrong and profane use of God's name has long been a common sin, but today it has become epidemic.

I remember the year quite well. It was 1976, our bicentennial year as a nation. This was the year that the major television companies began to introduce profanity, and especially the misuse of God's name, on a wide scale. One who worked in that industry told me that the new fall season was chosen as a test or gauge to see if the American public would tolerate widespread profanity on television. It seems that the idea was to measure the public reaction, and if the negative reaction was minimal, this would be an indication the viewing public was no longer offended by such language. Needless to say, the American public, at least as measured by the television audience, failed an important test without ever thinking twice about it.

So the name of God is being used irreverently and

blasphemously with impunity not only on TV but in the common everyday conversation among people. Before that fateful fall, the flippant and profane use of God's name was at least relatively rare … but no more. We are being blitzed by blasphemy. Human logic says, "Well if everyone is doing it, it mustn't really be too bad." Follow the same logic one step further in another direction to see the danger and absurdity of that kind of thinking. Since many people are going to hell, it must not be too bad a place to be. Does that help you see the folly of this sort of "logic"? The use of profanity, and especially the abuse of God's name, will do more to erode your character than any other one thing you do. It also reveals the true condition of your relationship with the Lord. It is hard to imagine that a person who has been pardoned from his sin by a holy yet merciful God will continue to abuse that dear and holy name.

This commandment also forbids and condemns the lack of reverence and the mocking of sacred things. The lack of a spirit of reverence is a serious symptom of a fatal malady. We must teach in every possible way respect and reverence for the name of God. This is done as we worship God according to His Word. This is one reason why it is so important to keep the house of God in good repair. This bears a testimony in the community. It also bears a negative testimony when churches are careless about the upkeep of their property. We properly rebuke our children for unseemly conduct in the church buildings. They need to know that the things of God are very special and very sacred. Reverence for all that is associated with the name of God is a high priority for every believer.

Another way in which we may take the name of God in vain is hypocrisy. This may be the most offensive manner of breaking this law in God's sight. The most crude and vulgar language of the street is not nearly so bad as the insincere profession of faith or the using of God's name in an insincere way. The commandment literally reads, "Thou shall not lift up the name of God in vanity."

You would agree that profanity is much more out of place in God's house than it is on the street, and you would agree that blasphemy, though terrible anywhere, would be especially heinous in a church; yet the prayer that is offered in God's house and in the name of God's Son that is not sincerely meant may be even more sinful than the blatant abuse of God's name. When we claim for ourselves the name "Christian" (Christ followers) and yet have no evidence of grace within our lives, we violate this law in a most serious way. In the early days of the Christian faith, believers were called Christians because they reminded people of Jesus Christ in their conduct. Do we remind this generation of Jesus Christ? If not, we break this law.

When Alexander the Great was leading his troops into battle, he told them that his good name depended upon their valor in battle, and he was entrusting to them his name for good or ill. This is just what the Lord Jesus Christ has done with us and with His name. He allows us to bear His name in this world for good or ill. Our conduct in the battles of life reflects upon the good name of our Lord Jesus Christ. We dare not take that precious and powerful name in vain. We may not like the responsibility, but the opinion that many will have of our Savior will depend upon their opinion of us. Think about that the next time you face dire temptation.

The kiss of Judas Iscariot and the word "master" with which he greeted the Lord when he betrayed him, was far more blasphemous — and a surer breaking of this commandment — than the mocking of the Roman soldiers, or even the taunting of the priests and scribes at His crucifixion. So, our calling Him "Lord" and yet denying or betraying Him by our conduct is more reprehensible than the cursing by the man who makes no claim of faith.

There is a positive side to this commandment. There is a right way to use His name, and by this law we are required to call upon His name in sincerity and to use it aright. God would have us use His name. He loves to hear His name in loving praise on the lips of His dear children. Even as a bride would constantly and lovingly speak of her husband, so will a Christian speak of her Lord or his Lord. It should be the most natural thing in the world for a Christian to use God's name; affectionately, reverently, and often.

The proper and reverent use of God's name will bear a witness to those who constantly abuse it. We should not blush to speak His name, and tell others what great things the Lord has done for us.

This law calls upon us to pray. What more proper way to use God's name than in prayer of praise or penitence? How wonderful it is to hear hundreds of believers every Lord's Day say: "Our Father, who art in heaven, hallowed be thy name." This commandment is also a call to song. Much of the language of Scripture is couched in verse, and many places in the Word command that we sing unto the Lord.

There is a broader implication involved in this command; it is the proper use of speech itself. The Bible warns against foolish and filthy talk. If we would but speak the name of our Lord as often as we speak words of complaining and words of gossip, how much better we and the world would be.

Above all, this law requires us to honor the precious name of our dear Savior. Our lives should bear a strong and winsome testimony to the credibility and sincerity of our profession. Just think! His name is the only thing standing between you and God's wrath. His name is your password into heaven. It is by His name you expect to face death. Should you not therefore honor that name which is above every name?

God need give no reason for His commands, for He is

the sovereign, omnipotent God who answers to none. Nevertheless, He has good reasons and reveals to us why we should obey Him. He promises blessings for obedience to all His commands, and warns of the consequence when we disobey. This law is no exception. Reason alone should tell us that this law is based on His goodness to us. He is our creator, sustainer, and redeemer. He holds our lives and our times in His hand. He gives the sunshine and the rain, the daily bread for both soul and body. In times of need and testing, He gives us grace and strengthens us with his blessed presence.

There is another reason. This is the only commandment with a specific warning: "The Lord will not hold him guiltless who takes His name in vain." To break this law tempts both the wrath and mercy of God. To break this law invites His judgment upon us. It wrecks our fellowship with Him and puts us in the company of scorners and mockers. That's bad company, especially when the company with God Himself is possible.

If you have found yourself in the spotlight of God's Word at this point, if the Holy Spirit has brought you into conviction because you have broken this law in some way either through careless speech or through an insincere profession, then why not this moment repent of this sin? Call upon His name; He is a merciful Father who freely forgives His erring children. He desires to hear you speak His name.

Talk to Him, thank Him for His name and all that it means. Take it, not in vain, but in truth and in grateful love.

"Thou shalt not take the name of the Lord thy God in vain." "O Lord, our Lord, how excellent is thy name in all the earth." "For there is no other name under heaven given among men whereby we must be saved."

ENDNOTES

[1] Exodus 20:7
[2] Psalm 8:1
[3] Matthew 6:9
[4] Acts 4:12
[5] John 17:4, 6
[6] Exodus 20:7
[7] Proverbs 14:9

FOR FURTHER STUDY

1. Westminster Larger Catechism Questions and Answers 111-114.
2. What is meant by God's "name"? Study John 17:6, 11-12:26.
3. What does it mean to pray in Jesus' name?
4. Using a good concordance, look up all Scripture references to God's names.
5. What are some possible ways to misuse God's name?
6. Is it ever right to swear by His name? (How about an oath in a court of law?)

Chapter 5

GOD'S HOLY DAY

"Remember the Sabbath day to keep it holy."[1] "The Sabbath was made for man, and not man for the Sabbath."[2] "… it is lawful to do good on the Sabbath."[3] These are words which teach that God has a special day in our lives set aside for Him, that this day was made for our good and blessing, and that we should keep it holy and wholly unto Him. Jesus' perfect example and His perfect interpretation of this commandment provides the key to our understanding of it, as well as our faithful obedience to it.

To get some idea of the importance of the Ten Commandments, and of each law within this code, we need to remember that God only gave ten. He might have given a hundred commandments or even a thousand commandments. But He gave us ten. And these ten provide the foundation for all law and government. The welfare and good of the human race depend upon a recognition of these basic principles and a faithful application of them in the laws that control and regulate the conduct of citizenry of all nations.

The Sabbath law is much older than Sinai; it is as old as creation itself, when God established the principle and gave the most striking example of it. He rested from all His labor on the Sabbath, and decreed a day of rest for mankind.

This may well be the least regarded of the Ten Commandments, even by Bible-believing Christians. There is little preaching on this theme. There is open endorsement of the commercialization of God's day. The Church has joined the unbelieving world in changing a holy day into a holiday. A careful study of Scripture, however, fails to reveal that God has repealed this law. In fact, it may well be one of the most important commandments. It is included in the section of the law which instructs us in our relationship to God. Therefore, it becomes a part of the first and great commandment to love the Lord our God with all heart, soul, mind, and strength.

Do you regard yourself as a patriotic American? Do you accept the role as a Christian patriot whose duty is to be the salt of the earth and the light of the world? If I understand the Old Testament rightly, then one of the most unpatriotic things you may ever do is to treat God's holy day lightly and fail in the command to keep it holy. Why do I say this? Of all the national sins which led to Israel's downfall as a nation, this is the one highlighted in Scripture. In fact, the length of the captivity, 70 years, was directly related to the time they had failed to observe the Sabbath principle. God blesses those who honor His day, and He punishes those who fail to do so.

Many Christians fail to see the importance of this commandment and beg to be excused from any obligation to it.

They seem to think that it is entirely a matter of one's own opinion and choice as to how God's day is to be kept. Would that also apply to other commandments, i.e., 6-7-8? Perhaps the manner in which this whole matter is discussed is the best indication of our attitude towards it. How many discussions about God's day have you ever heard in which the major concern was how we may honor God rather than what we can get away with doing. "What's wrong with …" is usually the way any conversation about Sabbath observation begins … and ends. Most people frankly say, "What I do with my weekend is my own business and nobody else's." This begs the issue. The real question is this: Is it "your weekend" or is it God's holy day? If you do believe it to be God's holy day, then it is proper and necessary that you understand what God requires by this law and how we may keep His day holy.

One of my early memories of a Sabbath day controversy had to do with a rat in the grain bin. I knew the Bible taught it was right to feed and care for the stock on the Sabbath, but I wasn't sure if that also included killing the rats who were eating the grain intended for the cow. When I asked permission from my dad to use my brand new BB gun to shoot the rat on Sunday, he said he wasn't sure whether it was a work of necessity or mercy, but by all means kill the rat.

In a more serious vein, one of the elders in the little Presbyterian church I attended as a boy, was faced with a moral decision concerning the Lord's Day. He was the father of a large family for whom he provided by following the trade of a carpenter. He found himself out of work in the early days of World War II. He was offered a job on a defense contract but turned it down on the basis it required him to work on the Lord's Day. Some said he was foolish, but he trusted God would honor those who honor Him. He soon had another job but, more importantly, he had a lasting reputation in our community as a man of principle and an elder of great worth in his church. I'm not at all sure church people today would appreciate the stand he made.

From the earliest days, when this law, which was inherent in creation, was formally given, there was resistance and rebellion to it. The Israelites in the wilderness tried the patience of God by ignoring His ban on manna-gathering on the Sabbath. During the times of the prophets, God complained against His people because they had turned His day into a commercial day, and even when they observed it they said, "When will the Sabbath be over that we might buy and sell?"[4] As previously noted, it was one of the major contributing factors in the downfall of Israel. This was not arbitrary. When man neglects God's day, or changes the intention and use of it away from worship and rest, his relationship with the Lord suffers.

Following the captivity, great importance was placed on the keeping of the Sabbath. By the time the Lord Jesus came to earth, an equally serious abuse of the Sabbath had developed among the Jews. An excessive and petty legalism, which had lost the original intention in a maze of interpretation and minutiae, had distorted the day into one of burdensome disregard of mercy and truth. Jesus was often accused of violating the Sabbath because He was willing to heal the sick and care for the needy on the Sabbath. This criticism offered Him the opportunity to teach the right kind of Sabbath observance both by example and precept. He restored its purpose as a day to honor the Lord by worship in God's house, but also by doing deeds of loving mercy to the sick and lame. He even allowed for deeds of necessity when His disciples were criticized for plucking and eating grains of wheat on the Sabbath. His teaching so enraged the self-righteous Pharisees that they sought to kill Him for His supposed violation of the Sabbath. When Jesus said the Sabbath was made for man, and not man for the Sabbath, He was saying it was made for him to have fellowship with God and to serve Him.

Let's examine some of the reasons why such a day has been set aside by God through His law. This day was given that we might acknowledge and worship our creator. Since we are created in the image of Him who rested on the Sabbath, the proper observation of this day is both necessary and logical. John Calvin said we should rest from our labor in order that God might do His work in us. Another reason this day was given was so that the world might recognize that we are God's people. This was one of the testimonies Israel bore in the ancient world. It is a testimony we may bear in our age. When God gave this law, He not only required that His people keep it holy, but that they refrain from work or requiring others to work for them.[5] So this law is intended to protect the working man from the tyranny of those who would exploit him.

    Since it is obvious that the Old Testament Sabbath was held on the seventh day of the week, why then do Christians keep the first day as the Christian Sabbath, and why have they done so ever since very early in New Testament times? We discover that Christians in the book of Acts were gathering on the first day to worship. Paul's letters make it very clear this was universal practice. The new creation in Christ began when the Lord was raised from the dead on the first day of the week. Apparently, Pentecost also took place on the first day. Not only does Paul speak of the first day as being the Christian day of worship, but John also records in the book of Revelation: "I was in the spirit on the Lord's Day …"[6] and on that glorious day, Christ revealed to him the glories recorded in that last book of the Bible. The unbroken history of the Church from that day to this records the universal acceptance of the transfer from seventh to first. Though this is disputed by isolated sects and cults, it should not greatly trouble the majority of us.

Though there is some minor disagreement on the day, there should be none on the principle that God requires one day for Himself set aside from toil and pleasures of the earth. Do you know there is a verse in the book of Isaiah which promised great blessings to those who turn aside from their work and pleasure on the Sabbath day, and take their pleasure in the Lord? He promised those who obey Him will ride on the high places of the earth and inherit the covenant promises He made with Jacob.

The Christian home is one of the foundation stones upon which our culture rests; the other is the Christian Sabbath. Both are in danger of destruction. The Church depends upon the Sabbath for its very life. Church history demonstrates that when the Christian Sabbath is weakened, the Church is weakened. When the Soviets took over Russia, they set out to destroy the Church. One of the weapons they used was the destruction of the Christian Sabbath. They largely succeeded in doing both. Much the same is happening right here in our own country. The secularists wish to destroy the influence of the Church on society and remove its irritating hindrance to the advance of secular humanism. So, the Christian Sabbath has become the target for attack under the guise of freedom and the separation of church and state. To a large degree, and enthusiastically aided by either naïve or rebellious Christians, the secularist has succeeded in the destruction of the Christian Sabbath as an American institution. His real purpose is to destroy any moral basis for conduct in any realm.

Without falling into the error of the Pharisee, may we note at least some guidelines for Christians to follow as they make their decisions about the Lord's Day?

It is biblical to do certain things on the Lord's Day. Worship is taught and commanded. There can be no reality of relationship with God when there is no worship of Him; and when there are not times set aside for worship, there will be no worship. It is important for believers to prepare themselves for worship before they come to God's house. If worship is dull and uninteresting for you, if you find yourself sleeping through the sermon and exhausted by the thought of sitting through a whole hour in church, the problem might begin with what you do on Saturday night. I would especially urge you fathers to order your household so that proper rest and preparation might be made in your family, that Sunday will not be a day of sleepy drudgery. What a difference between the one who worships God privately every day and joins with others to worship the Lord publicly, and the one who never has time for God during the week and only occasionally drags himself to church.

Service in the name and for the cause of Christ is another positive and proper use of our time on God's day. The example and teaching of Christ on this is all we need for motivation and warrant. We may do such deeds as necessity may require and charity demand. But we have to be careful that need is real and not mere desire or whim.

There must also be some "don't" principles. I am not talking about a list of petty details, but some guidelines. You must answer to God for what you do and don't do on His day. By all means, avoid the sullen defiant attitude which constantly cries, "What's wrong with what I want to do?" Rather, adopt a servant attitude of "Lord, how may I honor you on your day?" Another very important principle for you to work out in your life is this: don't contribute to the commercialization of God's day. This is one of the clearest teachings concerning this commandment. That means God would not have you work at your regular employment on His day. There may be some occupations in which the only "necessity" is to make more money. Ever since I have been in the ministry, I have been told by multitudes of people they have an ox in the ditch as an excuse for not attending church or for working on Sunday. Most of these folks have never seen an ox, let alone one that has fallen into a ditch. But allowing for the times when the "ox" is truly "in the ditch": If that happens on a regular basis, the best thing for you to do is either sell that clumsy ox before it hurts itself or you, or at least fill in the ditch … but not on Sunday.

Don't let popular opinion prevail over God's revealed will. Don't make the Lord's Day one in which you pursue selfish pleasure, for your play is the other man's work. If you seriously work at fleshing out these general principles, you will arrive at your own list of things to do and not do on God's day, and He will honor and bless you for it. If you are in error, He will show you.

Sunday can be the day of greatest blessings for believers if the example of Jesus is followed. Seek out the house and people of God that you might consider God's Word, and raise your voice in prayer and praise. Like the Lord, seek out the needy; nursing homes are full of them. Bring joy where there is sorrow, and sunshine where there is darkness. Seek out the straying and erring, and win them back to the kingdom. If true need requires you to work, do it as unto the Lord with gladness of heart and willingness of mind and hand. It's hard to go wrong when you consciously follow the footprints of Jesus. He is always going in the right direction on the Lord's Day and every day.

ENDNOTES

[1] Exodus 20:8
[2] Mark 2:27
[3] Matthew 12:12
[4] Amos 8:5
[5] Exodus 20:10
[6] Revelation 1:10

FOR FURTHER STUDY

1. Westminster Larger Catechism Questions and Answers 116-121.
2. Why is the Sabbath principle important to Christians?
3. What would constitute works of necessity?
4. In what sense was the Sabbath made for man?
5. Are our reasons for observing the first day of the week as the Christian Sabbath valid? Why or why not?
6. What is the essence of the promise in Isaiah 58:13-14?
7. Should Christians press for legislation that defends the Sabbath day?

Chapter 6

PARENTS — THEIR HONOR AND DUTY

The word of God commands, "Honor thy father and mother, that thy days may be long upon the land which the Lord thy God giveth thee."[1] "Children obey your parents in the Lord for this is right."[2] "Fathers provoke not your children to wrath, but bring them up in the nurture and admonition of the Lord."[3] The fifth commandment is the hinge commandment. It stands between the two tables of the law and binds them together, forming the bridge between our duty to God and our duty to man. Obedience to this law will go a long way towards loving God with all heart, mind, and strength, and loving your neighbor as yourself.

The purpose of this law was to lay a solid foundation upon which the family might rest. The family is the basic unit of society and it is the model and pattern after which all government is to be formed. This is true in Church and state. The elders in the Church are the spiritual fathers of God's flock. The elected officials in civil government ideally are as fathers to the population. Seldom is the ideal achieved, nevertheless God's intention for government is just this ideal. When Christ was on trial before godless Pontius Pilate, who was the representative of Roman power in Judea, he reminded proud Pilate that the only authority he possessed was from above.

The survival of true government depends upon the survival of the family unit, and the family survival depends upon obedience to this law. The prime reason why we are seeing the breakdown of authority and the chaos of disorderly conduct in our nation is the failure of the American family to function according to this law. The youth rebellion which began in the sixties and the radical feminist movement since that time have both sprung from a rejection of this law, and are the bitter fruit of man's attempt to free himself from God's authority.

Someone with a gift for poetical expression once said: "My son, all you are and have on earth you owe to your parents. They have given you life and thus have given you the privilege of seeing the majesty of the sun, the moon, the stars; the glorious beauty of the snow-capped hills, the blue ocean, and the endless beauty of the changing seasons." God's Word says, "Honor thy father and mother." Both Old and New testaments teach this truth and strongly emphasize its importance. Therefore, it is of utmost importance that we understand it and the implications of it for our lives today.

The passage from Ephesians 6 which quotes this commandment and elaborates on it demonstrates the much wider application of this law beyond the basic family unit. It applies to the relationship between employer and employee, and between the citizen and the state. This law really teaches respect for all forms of authority which God may place over us. In Peter's epistle, he points out that even though government may be unworthy of our respect, still it is God's agent of authority and must be obeyed. Of course, there are limits to this, and trying to discern those limits has been a matter of controversy down through history. For instance, both Patriots and Tories quote Scripture to justify their opposing positions on loyalty to the British crown during the American revolution. In more recent history, Christians in Nazi Germany faced many hard decisions on this thorny issue. Some resisted the government's efforts to exterminate the Jews and paid for it with their own lives. Others bowed to government pressure and found themselves with blood on their hands because they did not resist the mass genocide. In even more recent years, we saw many American youths refuse to register for the draft on the grounds they might have to fight in wars they considered morally wrong, though at the same time they eagerly accepted government handouts for their education and saw no contradiction in doing so.

Incidentally, the Ten Commandments have a unique feature here that none of the other ancient codes of law included: a requirement that mothers share in the honor accorded fathers. Some other codes commanded obedience and respect for fathers, but in God's law, the mother is elevated to a position of equal respect and honor in the sight of children. In fact, in one of the places where this law is repeated in the Old Testament, the order is reversed and children are called upon to obey mothers and fathers. The ancient Jewish rabbis saw this as an indication God required equal honor and respect for both parents. This requires fathers to set the example by holding their wives in highest respect, and showing by example that the children must also respect and obey their mothers. It is the father's duty to support his wife when she corrects and disciplines the children, and never show disrespect for her, especially before the children.

    Now let's begin to examine more closely the teachings of this law. What does it require? What duties does it demand of God's people? First of all, it teaches the duty of parents to their children. The honor and obedience required of children flows from the character and behavior of parents. God requires that parents be spiritual leaders and instructors of their children. This is most vividly seen in the baptismal vows believing parents take on behalf of their children. They claim God's grace for them and then go on to make certain covenant promises of things they will do for and with their children, including prayer with and for them, the setting of a godly example, and instruction in the doctrines of faith. When the Christian parent takes these vows, it is an expression of obedience to this law. Your children's basic concepts of God will come from you, both by instruction and example. Their perception of who God is and what He is like will be based on their relationship with you. That is an awesome responsibility. It should serve to keep parents on their knees. What are you teaching your children about God? Do they see in your life that God is really important, that He comes first? Do they see in your life that God changes people, that He forgives and gives power to forgive? Or do they learn that other things are more important, that pleasure and profit both come before God? Our children will listen to our words to an extent, but they will follow our example more than they will heed our instructions. When there is wide variance between what we teach them by word and what we teach them by example, they will be confused and resentful.

Don't get the wrong idea; a good example, though extremely important, is by itself not enough. The Bible commands that we teach our children by precept as well. We are to tell them who God is, what He has done for us poor sinners, and how we may have salvation by trusting His Son. We are to warn them that the wages of sin is death, but also to encourage them to know that if we confess our sins, He is faithful and just to forgive our sins and to cleanse us from all unrighteousness. We are to make sure they learn the basic messages of the Bible. This will require much time spent in Bible reading and Bible story time. It will require that we give up time spent in other ways, both for the parent and the child. Before a child goes off to school in the first grade, he should be thoroughly grounded in God's Word. Impossible? Not at all to the parent who understands the implication of this commandment and undertakes to fulfill it. Our children should be more familiar with the stories of the Bible than they are with the stories of the founding of our country. They should know the Bible better than they know Mother Goose or Dr. Seuss.

This commandment teaches the duty of godly love. I emphasize godly love because not all parental love is godly love. Some of it is frankly selfish. Parents try to live out their ambitions through their children. It saddens me to know that some Christian young people are stifled in their religious impulses by parents who are overly ambitious for them to succeed in sports, social standing, or scholastic achievements. This is not a rare thing at all; in fact, it is all too common. There are some parents who wish to totally dominate their children and turn them into clones of themselves.

I know parents who seem to specialize in making their children feel guilty. Some people go through life troubled, vexed, and warped because their parents have made them feel guilty about anything that does not put the will of the parent first. Parental selfishness is a poor substitute for godly parental love. Do not baptize your selfishness by calling it parental love. Do not hide behind this commandment to force your will on your children; rather, strive to teach them God's will. Selfish parental love is one of the most destructive forces in the world. Let your love for your children follow the example and pattern of God's love for you, and be a love that will bring them to experience and practice God's love in their lives.

There is also the duty of discipline. Discipline must begin at home, and if it does not, it will not be possible in school or in society at large. In both school and pubic life, we are reaping the bitter fruit of the "Dr. Spock" generation. Now for all the good and helpful things Dr. Spock might have said in his books about child rearing, nevertheless, his idea that children should be allowed to develop their own personalities in freedom from restraint by parents is most destructive of law and order at every level. The child who is not properly disciplined by parents will probably never learn self-discipline, and may well become a danger to society. Discipline is costly for the parents. It is emotionally draining, exhausting, and it takes much time. It wears and tears, but oh how necessary it is. Dr. G. Campbell Morgan, a great preacher in the early part of the 20th century, raised five sons who were ministers. It was said at a family gathering late in Dr. Morgan's life that his sons were chiding him for being too strict on them in childhood. His reply was: "When you each have raised five sons for the ministry as I have done, then return and instruct me in how I should have raised you."

This is a must if you are to fulfill the requirements of God in this law. The book of Proverbs says, "He who spares the rod hates his child."[4] How true! Look at the tragic examples in Scripture of men who failed to properly discipline their sons. Three generations of great men one after another failed miserably in this. Eli, the priest, failed to discipline his sons for profaning the temple and priesthood. For this, he was severely rebuked and punished by the death of his sons. Samuel, who was sent by God to warn Eli of his failure, and who saw the tragic end of Eli's sons, nevertheless also failed to discipline his sons, and heard the people of Israel demand a king because his sons did not walk in his ways. Samuel anointed David to be king over Israel, and David, too, failed in this important task. His failure resulted in terrible things within his own household: rape, incest, fratricide, rebellion, and loss of respect.

Discipline means more than punishment for wrongdoing; it involves rewards for rightdoing and encouragement in rightdoing. Martin Luther said: "Keep both the rod and the apple handy when you discipline your child." Failure to do this is just as destructive as failure to punish for wrongdoing.

In one of the Old Testament lists of kings and their achievements, this comment is made about one of the most wicked of all the kings: "… his mother was his counselor for evil."[5] What a sad epitaph to be written into the stones of history. In this case, it was a deliberate attempt by the king's mother to turn him away from God, but it would be possible for well-meaning parents to become "counselors for evil," especially in the matter of example. For the duty of example is also a part of this law. For good or ill, most children will be very much like their parents. I remember once at a summer church camp telling a group of teen-aged boys that if they wished to know what their girlfriends would be like in twenty years, just look at their mothers. That ended some beautiful summer romances! It would be a mistake to push this idea too far, else we would rule out the grace and power of God to transform lives, but at the same time, experience shows that in most cases children become very much like their parents.

The other side of this commandment has to do with the duty children owe their parents. After all, this is what the law speaks to most directly. What do you owe your parents? First, obedience. Obedience is the first law of love for God and for parents. Jesus said, "If you love me keep [obey] my commandments." The same thing is true of parents. If you love your parents, obey them. This is the path to honor and peace. This is the first giant step towards a right relationship with God. The apostle Paul placed disobedience to parents in the same category as murder, stealing, witchcraft, truce breaking, and other similarly heinous sins.[6] Paul went on to describe this sin as being one of the characteristics of the last days when law and order break down and iniquity reigns. In fact, in the Old Testament, this was one of the sins for which capital punishment might be applied. Why was this so? It is because the whole fabric of life among God's people depended upon the sanctity and structure of the family. Rebellion against parental authority is rebellion against God, and rebellion against God leads to destruction. Malachi warns of the curse of God on earth because the hearts of children and parents are against each other. [7]

Obedience must also include respect. Can you think of anyone who has greatly benefited mankind who did not respect his parents? Jesus submitted Himself to the authority of earthly parents even though He knew He was the Son of God. I think one of the greatest men in American history was George Washington. He was known as a man who respected and honored his country, an attitude which first expressed itself toward his parents. At one point, he was ready to go to sea and become a sailor, but he respected his mother's wish and remained at home. God honored such honor. This respect and honor for parents should be not only for their persons but for their standards and wishes. As a child, you may consider your parents old-fashioned and hopelessly out of touch with the times, but the chances are they are much nearer the will of God than you are. Your rebellion against them may only be an expression of your rebellion against God's Word. Godliness is never old-fashioned, but sin is a serious problem in every generation. Your parents are not nearly as unreasonable, ignorant, and uneducated as you think they are.

Very often, as a pastor, I am asked, "How can I

possibly honor my parents when they are so old-fashioned, so mean and unreasonable, so sinful and selfish?" I know that can be a very difficult situation because these things may well be true. May I remind you of something Jesus said which may help? He said we are to love our enemies, to bless those who curse you, do good to those who hate you and despitefully use you. How much more, then, should you love and honor parents who, with all their faults, would still gladly die for you? You may protest that your parents are unworthy of your love, and this may be true, but you, too, have a multitude of sins to be forgiven, and none of us are worthy of God's love. Then, too, parents are usually the only people in all the world who will ever love you unconditionally. They love you not for what you do or don't do, but because you are their child. They love you more than you will ever love them or anyone else until you have children of your own to love. No man ever loves his father as much as he loves his son, and this is how God arranged it.

    Just as parents have a duty to love their children with all godly love, so children have a like duty towards their parents. As children, ours should be a love born of gratitude, and this love should not end with the passing of years or changing of circumstances. In fact, our love for our parents, like our love for God, should grow with the years. Never, never be ashamed of your parents because they have come from humble circumstances or are poor and uneducated.

Perhaps some of their poverty is because they sacrificed their own future security that you might have an education. I can remember as a young boy being ashamed that my parents did not have as much as some I knew. I can remember not wanting to sit with them in church, but no more. I am thankful God placed me in the care of such Christian people, and hope to do as well by my children as they did by theirs.

There is a promise in Jeremiah 35 to which everyone should aspire. The Rechabites were chosen by God as a rebuke to unfaithful Judah, which had broken its covenant vows to God. They were descendants of a man who had vowed that neither he nor his offspring would ever drink wine. Jeremiah brought them into the house of God and set wine before them and bade them drink. They refused because of the vow of their father. Jeremiah cited their steadfastness to their father's vow in sharp contrast to the men of Judah who ignored the vows of their fathers and their own. "They have obeyed their father's command, but I have spoken to you again and again, and you have not listened to me," God complained against Judah. Then to the Rechabites God said, "Because you have obeyed the command of Jonadab, your father, kept all his commands … therefore thus says the Lord of hosts, the God of Israel, 'Jonadab, son of Rechab, shall not lack a man to stand before me forever.'"

What did Jesus teach about this law? "Suffer the little children to come unto me, and forbid them not…"[8]

In another place, He talked about how earthly fathers delight to give good things to their children. "If your son asks for an egg, will you give him a stone?..."[9] By these words our Lord was teaching the primary duties of parents towards their children. First, to bring them to Him. This speaks of the spiritual leadership parents exercise in their homes. Our first and greatest task is to give our children back to God as mature believers who love and honor Him. Secondly, we are to provide for their material and physical needs. Of course, in context He was teaching more than these things as well, but certainly these two duties are incumbent on every parent.

Two other passages serve to underscore his teachings as to the duties children owe their parents. When the Lord Jesus was a young boy, He went to the temple with His parents. During their stay there, He became separated from them and remained behind when they left for home. When they went back to Jerusalem to look for Him, they found Him in the temple conversing with the rabbis on Scripture. His parents rebuked Him for this, and even though He replied, "Did you not know that I must be about my father's business," He gladly returned with them to Nazareth and submitted to their authority.[10] In another place, Jesus cited the evil practice of Corban as an example of the way some were failing to care for their aged and needy parents.[11] His teaching in each case is very clear. Young children are to submit to the authority of their parents, and in later years are to care for them in their need.

Maybe the most important thing that has ever been said about parenthood is to be found in the words of the Lord Jesus when He said to His disciples: "When you pray, say Our Father, who are in heaven ..." Here is our example, and here is our hope. It is possible for a sinful person to become a child of the heavenly father. He will adopt you as His own dear child if you will believe in and accept His Son as your savior. Your faith in Christ honors the Father in heaven, which is the highest form of obedience to the command which says, "Honor thy father and thy mother ..."

ENDNOTES

[1] Exodus 20:12
[2] Ephesians 6:1
[3] Ephesians 6:4
[4] Proverbs 13:24
[5] II Chronicles 22:3
[6] II Timothy 3:2
[7] Malachi 4:6
[8] Matthew 19:14
[9] Luke 11:12
[10] Luke 2:41-52
[11] Mark 7:10-14

FOR FURTHER STUDY

1. Westminster Larger Catechism Questions and Answers 123-133.
2. Why is this commandment so important in our relationship to God? and to man?
3. What is the purpose of this law?
4. What are some New Testament passages which bear on this commandment?
5. How far should we go in obedience to godless parents?
6. How far should we go in obedience to godless government?
7. How might parents provoke their children to wrath?
8. How may they avoid this?
9. How is discipline an expression of love?

Chapter 7

MY BROTHER'S KEEPER

This commandment of God is very straight-forward and direct, "Thou shalt not kill."[1] It teaches the sanctity of life and the terrible sin of committing murder. Even on the surface of it, we are living in a world and in a time when this law is ignored and broken to a shocking extent in a variety of ways. In the eyes of many people, human life is dreadfully cheap. Several years ago, a man sat in my office with a troubled mind. His married daughter was involved in an affair with a man of another race. He was hurt and angry. He was tempted by an offer that had come through an acquaintance who had heard of the situation. For only $500, murder could be committed and no questions asked. What really troubled this man was the strong temptation this presented to him.

This is not as far removed from our lives as we would like to think. Recently, the newspaper carried a story of young teenage girl who had been brutally murdered. For several days, the murder went unreported, even though a number of the boys in her high school had seen her body lying in the underbrush near the school. It had almost become a game to slip out and see her dead body before it was finally reported to the police. When asked why they had failed to report this ghastly deed to the police, the young fellows replied they just did not want to be involved.

God has commanded, "Thou shalt not murder," and this law has never been revoked. In the age in which this law was first given, it was sorely needed. The tragedy of Cain and Abel had long since been forgotten. The instructions to Noah, "Whoso sheds man's blood, by man shall his blood be shed,"[2] had also been laid aside. As now, so then, life was cheap. Moses, through whom the law was given, had barely escaped with his life while still a helpless infant. Wicked Pharaoh had decreed that all male babies of the Hebrews were to be thrown into the Nile. Only the faith and courage of his parents had saved Moses' life. Is this shocking scene of infanticide any more terrible than the wholesale slaughter of the unborn in our own nation? How many millions have been killed? Who is responsible for this unbelievable tragedy?

In the age of Moses, a master might kill his slave without accountability for it. Kings frequently killed messengers who brought bad news. The ancient world desperately needed to hear God's thunder from Mount Sinai, "Thou shalt not kill." Is our modern world in any less need? Who are we to cast stones at another generation? Our own indifference towards murder is undeniable. We have become so used to stories of violent death that we are almost immune to shock. A young man was murdered while serving a prison sentence for a relatively minor offense, but public reaction was less than overwhelming. "He got what he deserved. He shouldn't have been there in the first place," was one comment reported.

Much concern for human life is either selfish, hypocritical, or non-existent. Why are we so unconcerned about the loss of life that doesn't directly affect us? Where is the radical left in our country who were willing to tear the nation apart to protest the Vietnam War, but have been utterly silent about the massacre of millions which has occurred since our withdrawal from that area? Another even more embarrassing question is why do some Christians cry out against the mass murder of the unborn but remain silent about the massacre of 10,000 teenagers each year by drunken drivers? Why is it that all-night vigils will be held to protest the rightful execution of a mass murderer, and little, if any, concern will be shown towards his many victims? Those who use the commandment to protest capital punishment are ignoring the Bible's own interpretation of this law; in fact, the scriptures teach that God requires capital punishment in some cases.

What does this law teach? How are we to obey it? How may it be broken? These are important and sometimes complicated questions which need an answer. Let's look first at how this law may be broken. Quite obviously, this law forbids outright premeditated murder. Long before the commandment was formally given, it was wrong to murder. Cain discovered this to his own hurt. God said to him, "Your brother's blood cries out from the ground."[3] Cain was warned, but ignored that warning. We should take God's warning to Cain seriously. "Sin lieth at the door"[4] when we allow hatred to dominate our thinking towards another person.

We may also break this command by neglect and indifference. If I know my neighbor is in danger or in great need and do nothing about it, I am guilty of breaking this law. If I see my neighbor's house afire and do not warn him and he perishes in the blaze, am I not guilty? The person who deliberately drives in a careless manner, ignoring laws of safety and speed, or who drives under the influence of drugs or alcohol may be guilty of murder. This law speaks against self-destruction. Suicide is one form of murder. What about the company that works a man to death? That company and those in charge of it are guilty before God.

Jesus used this law as an example of how one must not only obey the direct teaching of the law, but must also search out the intention and spirit behind the law in order to give it full obedience. When we take seriously what Jesus said, we discover it is one of the most difficult laws to obey and one most easily broken. According to Christ, anger, hatred, and contempt of another leaves one guilty of breaking this commandment.[5] He warned against these attitudes which lead to murder and make one guilty of violating the intention of this law. In another place we are warned, "Guard your heart diligently, for out of it are the issues of life."[6] Here the battle is won or lost, attitude leads to action. Behind the angry hatred of another person there is a prior sin. It is an unforgiving spirit. This blocks the work of God's spirit in your life. An unforgiving spirit carefully nourished and cherished may well lead to crimes of violence and even to murder. There are other steps along this dangerous path. Envy is one. If I am envious of my fellow man, I may give way to a smoldering, lingering resentment, and even to hatred. If I allow the spirit of revenge and retaliation to control my heart, I may be overwhelmed by these things, even to the point of justifying injury and death to my fellow man.

There are other issues which must be decided in light of this commandment. Euthanasia is being actively discussed today as a viable alternative to lingering illness and old age. The other side of this same issue is the matter of artificial extension of life by medical means. These are some of the questions raised in considering this commandment. Each of us must think through the answers to these with help of the principles shown to us in God's Word and especially in this commandment.

Equally important to the question, "How may I break this law?" is the question, "How may I keep this law?" The answer to this question must take in the spirit and intention of the law as well as the letter. Above all, the basic teaching of this commandment is, I am my brother's keeper. I am responsible for his life and his welfare. Life is a sacred trust from God, my own life and my neighbor's life. Therefore, I must take all reasonable and necessary steps to protect and preserve his life and mine. This commandment lays upon me the duty to do all I may as an individual to express my responsibilities to my neighbor, but also to join with others in the support of laws and means to protect and defend life. Obedience to this law requires my support of just laws which protect the innocent and punish the guilty, especially those guilty of murder and other violent crimes.

There is, however, an even higher duty towards this commandment. According to Scripture, life in its fullest expression is a right relationship to God and, ultimately, death is to be cut off from Him. This was the meaning behind God's warning to Adam, "In the day you sin, you will surely die."[7] We must never forget that all people apart from a saving relationship with God through Jesus Christ are under the sentence and curse of death forever. For a believer in Jesus Christ to deny that, or to act as if it were not true, is to commit a dreadful sin. We would all rise up and condemn a doctor who refused to treat a dying person, or who would turn away a cry for help. How much more reprehensible it is for Christians to ignore the dreadful condition of the spiritually dying and offer no help, withholding the only remedy for their condition. We would quickly condemn the one who stands idly by watching another die when it is within his power to help, but do we not stand idly by while many die without a knowledge of salvation? When God spoke to His servant Ezekiel as recorded in chapter 33 of that book, He told him to speak to the wicked and warn him from his ways. If Ezekiel was faithful to this charge though the wicked did not repent, nevertheless he would be innocent of the blood of the wicked. But if Ezekiel failed to warn the wicked, God would hold him accountable for their death.[8] Surely we are charged with similar responsibility and will be held accountable for it. Even as the blood of Abel cried out to God from the ground, so the heart cry of the lost to whom we have failed to witness comes up before the God who said, "Thou shalt not kill."

ENDNOTES

[1] Exodus 20:13
[2] Genesis 9:6
[3] Genesis 4:10
[4] Genesis 4:7
[5] Matthew 5:22
[6] Proverbs 4:23
[7] Genesis 2:17
[8] Ezekiel 33:8

FOR FURTHER STUDY

1. Westminster Larger Catechism Questions and Answers 134-136.
2. What can Christians do to combat the wholesale murder of unborn infants?
3. How may we refute the accusation that capital punishment is murder?
4. Is war forbidden by this commandment?
5. How might an unforgiving spirit lead to murder?
6. Does the Bible differentiate in degrees of murder? Cite specific passages.
7. What did Jesus teach about this commandment in Matthew 5:21-26?

Chapter 8

PURITY IN HEART AND LIFE

In spite of all our frantic efforts to ignore or negate this commandment of God, it remains clear and powerful. Let me remind you again of an important principle of interpretation in understanding the Ten Commandments. The purpose of God's law is not to be understood as a code which forbids the fulfillment of our human nature. We are not to think of these laws as primarily telling us what to do or not do, so much as pointing us in the direction of a successful and happy life. None of the commandments illustrates this truth more perfectly than the seventh: "Thou shalt not commit adultery."[1] For all the sins forbidden by this commandment seem to offer happiness, freedom, contentment, and fulfillment. Deluded by this false thinking, modern man has abandoned the commandment and has embraced immorality as an acceptable way of life. What do we find? Rather than being able to fulfill all the apparent promises, this way of life leads instead to misery, bondage, and living death, including separation from the one true source of love — God. In the name of love, many have cut themselves off from Love.

> "In vain we call old notions fudge,
> and bend our conscience to our dealing;
> the Ten Commandments will not budge,
> and stealing will continue stealing."

And adultery will continue to be adultery whatever the opinion of man.

Once again, we see the primary purposes of the law, which are to convict, convert, and teach holy living. Is there any law so flaunted and rejected as this one? Is there any law so necessary? Because he has ignored this law, modern man is wrapped in the chains of bondage. At the same time, he protests, "I am free, I am happy."

Any discussion of morality or marriage, any discussion of sex, any discussion of the relation between man and woman, must begin and be guided by the principle of this law. Any time we try to discuss these matters apart from the guidance of this commandment, we fall into error. The present moral tone of our nation cries out for this clear word from God. There is a great need for those who will stand upon this truth and will admit no compromise. Only these people offer any light and guidance out of the moral darkness, or any hope of finding a better way. If believers compromise this truth, we only serve to increase the darkness and hopelessness of humanity. When Jesus said to His disciples, "you are the light of the world,"[2] surely He included this.

When one begins to think of the terrifying statistics of broken homes, ruined marriages, blighted lives, confused children — not to mention such things as venereal diseases, teenage pregnancies, rape, and other crimes of sex — it is truly appalling. What lies at the root of these problems?

The rejection of God's law. We see this in so-called realism in books, movies, and television. We see this in a broad acceptance of the "new morality" which is old immorality with a new name. Isn't it absurd to call the kind of filth and trash which constantly is pandered upon the public, "adult entertainment"? Whatever else it is, it is not adult or mature. If this is the meaning of adulthood, may we all be babes and little children! In the midst of all this confusing, degrading current, there stands a rock: the Word of God. There is a pure stream which remains unpolluted by the world: the truth of the seventh commandment. God does not compromise His truth to accommodate the changing standards of fallen man.

What does this commandment teach? To what things does it say 'no'? All impurity of thought, word, or deed is forbidden by this law. It condemns all sex outside of marriage, regardless of how glamorous and exciting it can be made to sound. It forbids all violent crimes of sex. It disapproves all those wrong relationships which the world has sanctioned. It narrows the field of permissible divorce to the clear-cut guidelines of Scripture. This law does allow for divorce, and Jesus, as well as Paul, makes this clear, but it does not sanction the wholesale divorce rate we see today, nor the flimsy excuses for it which have become the modern code. For the Christian living today, surrounded by all sorts of ideas and thoughts about divorce and remarriage, there is a responsibility to search out all that Scripture has to say about these things, and make heartfelt commitment to the truth.[3]

A few years ago, the sin of homosexuality would not even be mentioned in decent print, nor spoken aloud — certainly not in church. Today it has become a burning issue within and without the church. It has become a major political issue in some cities and states. There are people who actually claim that it is an acceptable lifestyle, that it must not be called wrong. Some churches have ordained men and women who openly admit to the active practice of homosexuality, and some well-known church leaders have stoutly defended such actions as being consistent with Christian toleration. However, nothing has changed with God. These things are still condemned by the Word of God, and all such relationships invite the wrath of God, and stand forbidden by the seventh commandment.

This law also forbids those thoughts or actions which lead towards the overt breaking of the commandment. The battle is won or lost in the inner citadel of your heart. Jesus made that abundantly clear when He discussed this commandment in His Sermon on the Mount. After the Japanese attack on Pearl Harbor in 1941, the strategy of our armed forces was to carry the attack to the enemy. They did not plan to wait for the next blow to fall closer to home. There was no plan to take a stand on the west coast or the Mississippi River; that would have invited defeat. So you must not wait to do battle with this sin until the last desperate moment; you must defend the outer strongholds. You must beware of situations and conditions which might lead you astray.

The German high command fully realized that their war would be won or lost on the beaches that fateful D-Day of long ago, and had not Hitler interfered, they would have thrown all their might into those battles.

The battle for a pure mind and pure life requires the whole armor of God employed early. The defense perimeter must be well kept if victory is desired. Of the many scores of people with whom I have counseled who were involved in sexual sins, I can only recall two or three who confessed to a deliberate premeditated breaking of this commandment. Most of those counseled never intended for things to go as far as they did. Most never really meant to break God's law. It was a matter of a little carelessness here and compromise there, and the pattern of purity began to slip and the compromise of conscience became more and more serious until disaster fell. The accumulative effects of too much questionable literature, too many impure movies, too many ungodly friends wore down the sharp edges of discernment between right and wrong till wrong prevailed.

God's purpose behind the letter of the law is that we might be pure in heart and attitude. This is not easy, and a price must be paid for a pure heart before God. Jesus indicated that no price was too high for such a treasure.

Remember His words: "If your right eye offends you, pluck it out and cast it away ... If your right hand offends you, cut it off and cast it away ..."[4] Jesus was not teaching self-mutilation as the way to purity; He was teaching the costliness of purity. It is a battle not easily won. Perhaps you have some cherished and nurtured sin which is leading you into impurity. Maybe there is a relationship with another that you call innocent that borders on deadly peril. If so, these words of Jesus are meant for you. There are dangerous shoals ahead upon which you may make shipwreck of your life. Don't let it happen. Cut off those things and cast them away, lest you are caught in the hell of immorality. Evil thoughts and desires are always present within. The battle must be renewed every day. You can no more prevent unclean thoughts from going through your mind than you can keep birds from flying over your head, but you can keep birds from building a nest in your hair, and you can keep those thoughts from finding a permanent lodging place.

    One of the curses of America is the proliferation of impurity in language. Have you ever known a time when dirty language and filthy jokes were as commonplace as they are today? It's almost impossible to watch a television program without hearing obscenity and suggestive language. Look on any bestseller list of books and you will find most of them would be an embarrassment in your home. Christian men, do you bring lewd and dirty magazines into your home?

Is that what you want for your sons? Is that what you want your daughter to be like, a sex symbol for all to gaze upon? Loose language and loose living go hand in hand. Impure words and thoughts lead to impure lives; don't be naïve about this.

The seventh commandment has a positive side to it, and we need to be even more aware of this. The first step in understanding this positive teaching is to know that God created man, male and female, in His own image. God ordained sex and marriage as a part of man's nature, and the relationship between husband and wife with all its beautiful intimacy is a reflection of the triune nature of God. From Him, we learn the meaning of love in the fullest sense

It is required that we learn the difference between love and lust, between love and self-gratification, and because many people confuse these things they are led astray. This commandment requires of a man that he love his wife with a fervency of spirit and a purity of heart that is a reflection of God's love for Him. His example of love is the example we must follow.

The Scripture teaches that a man is to love his wife, even as Christ loved the Church and gave Himself for it.[5] It is no accident that the Church is called Christ's bride; it is an expression that has great bearing on this commandment. When Paul was explaining the kind of mutual love and submission a husband and wife owe each other, he couched his instructions in the language of Christ's love for the church. Christ gave himself for and to His bride, the Church; so must the husband do the same for his wife. He must love her so completely and unselfishly that there is no room for another. When Paul required the wife to submit herself to her own husband as unto the Lord, the accent may be upon the word, "own." For the loving wife, there is no room for another man. We may love many people, but never in the same intimate sense that husband and wife are to love each other. The gift of sex is a sacred trust, guarded and watched over by God's law. Therefore, we, too, must stand guard over it. By this pure law, we who are Christians are required to stand for decency and morality in the community, state, and nation. We are to search out and support those political candidates who are willing to take a similar stand. We are to speak out boldly against impurity and be willing to endure the anger and scorn of the world.

If we are to truly obey this law, then we must cultivate love for God so that all lesser loves will be controlled and governed by this. Yet, at the same time, this law warns us against the kind of self-righteousness and arrogance that would, with the Pharisee, take delight in exposing those who are trapped by this sin and bring them for stoning. Jesus would have nothing to do with their hypocritical efforts, and challenged the one among them without sin to cast the first stone.[6]

This law requires that when a brother or sister be overtaken with fault, the spiritual should restore such a one in the spirit of humility.[7] It forbids the kind of vanity that would cause me to enter God's house and pray, "God, I thank thee that I am not as other men," but rather it causes me to beat upon my breast and cry out, "God be merciful to me, the sinner."[8]

There are other considerations about this commandment which are important to its understanding and to our obedience. It is a sin against God. When David fell prey to adultery, he finally confessed to God, "against thee, thee only, have I sinned and done this evil in thy sight."[9] When Joseph was tempted by Potipher's beautiful wife, he resisted on the grounds this would be sin against God. No one else would ever know, but God
would know and so would Joseph, so he stood.[10]

This is especially a sin against Jesus Christ, God incarnate. Why? Because Christ has joined Himself to His people as head of the Body. Paul spoke of this in his letter to the Corinthians. "What, do you not know that your bodies are members of Christ? Shall I then take the members of Christ and make them members of an harlot? God forbid! ... Flee therefore immorality ... do you not know that your body is the temple of the Holy Spirit who is with you ...?"[11] So by this sin, we sin against the Lord Jesus Christ, the Holy Spirit who is within, and against our own selves. Is it really worth it? Are you really willing to join the name of Christ to such conduct? One of the most tragic consequences of immorality is divorce. The resulting breakup of families creates chaos. Ours is a nation destroying itself with this sin. Have you ever considered how confused young children must be? Have you ever thought what it must do to a child who owes allegiance to two households? No wonder they are having a terrible problem finding themselves; they don't really know who they are, and whose they are. We say these things with tenderness and heartbreak.

Adultery bears a bitter fruit and the surest of all harvests. The life of David is again a sad illustration. How he wept over his infant son born of Bathsheba, dying while still a babe. How much more bitter were the tears he shed over Absalom, his rebellious son who tried to steal the throne and was killed in the attempt. His tears were all the more bitter because David knew that Absalom's character lay upon his own conscience. David weeping was really David reaping what he had sown.

The inner destruction of character which this sin brings is devastating. Perhaps the worst form of this judgment is the loss of a reliable conscience. How frightening it must be to the pilot of a large airliner to lose his radar in a storm. How lost one feels in fog on the ocean without a compass. I know; it happened to me once and it still haunts me. Much worse is the person lost in the sea of immorality and impurity without a reliable conscience. Guard your heart, screen your mind lest it be filled with trash and rubbish. When you drift into sinful thoughts or words, confess quickly and seek cleansing. God will forgive and cleanse. Don't make the first compromise, then you will not have to worry about the next. Stay close to the holy God who loves you. When you break this law, you break his heart. "Grieve not the spirit of God whereby you are sealed unto the day of redemption."[12] If this law has brought conviction, may it also drive you to the Savior, who said to one of old whose life had been ruined by this sin, "neither do I condemn you, go and sin no more."[13]

Stand guard; you are not immune to this evil, nor are you above the temptation. God's guidepost stands close by the way. It warns of rough and dangerous roads, but points to the way of righteousness which leads to life eternal.

ENDNOTES

[1] Exodus 20:14 [2] Matthew 5:14

[3] John Murray's book *Divorce and Remarriage* is one work serious students of this matter should read. There are others.

[4] Matthew 5:29-30 [5] Ephesians 5:25 [6] John 8:7
[7] Galatians 6:1 [8] Luke 18:9-14 [9] Psalm 51:4
[10] Genesis 39:9 [11] I Corinthians 6:15-20 [12] Ephesians 4:30
[13] John 8:11

FOR FURTHER STUDY

1. Westminster Larger Catechism Questions and Answers 137-139.
2. Why is adultery a sin against God? See I Corinthians 6:15-19.
3. Is all sex outside marriage covered by this law?
4. Look up the passages in the Bible which refer to God's wrath against those who break this commandment, especially in the New Testament epistles and Revelation.
5. What did Jesus mean in Matthew 5:27-37?
6. Does the Scripture ever allow for divorce? On what grounds?

Chapter 9

DEALING WITH STEALING

The sin of stealing has become a national epidemic and a national disgrace. It threatens to undermine our whole social and economic fabric. Yet stealing, along with all its associated sins of dishonesty, has become so deeply ingrained into our way of life that many may be guilty of this without fully understanding the extent to which they have surrendered to this evil. It would be possible to simply list the many ways in which God's command, "Thou shalt not steal," is broken and fill page after page in this book. I will not do this for at least two reasons. First, I might give you some wrong ideas, and, secondly, you might begin to wonder about me. "How did you get to be such an expert on sin," you might ask.

Though I do not have actual statistics to quote, it is safe to say that stealing is the most commonly committed crime in our nation, and perhaps worldwide. Stealing lies at the root of many other crimes, especially crimes of violence — leading to injury and loss of life in many cases. Armed robbery has become so commonplace that it scarcely deserves an item in the newspaper. Pick up the morning newspaper of almost any city in America on any given day, and you will read of an armed robbery which has resulted in death or serious injury.

There are many other forms of stealing which also violate God's commandment. Recently, there was an unexpected snowstorm in one of our large southern cities which left thousands of commuters stranded, as well as many travelers on the interstate highway. The innkeepers and motel managers reaped a bonanza by taking advantage of the situation to charge as much as ten times the normal rate for their rooms. It is indisputable that any time we take such unfair advantage of our neighbor's distress, we are guilty of breaking the eighth commandment.

Do you realize that literally thousands of small and even large businesses have been forced out of business because of stealing? This stealing may be done by the employees, and even by the employer in some cases. Stealing may take the form of shoplifting (which is an euphemism for outright stealing), or it may take the form of customers refusing to pay their debts on time. I have talked to some men who have been forced out of business because the U.S. government has failed to pay for services, even after repeated billing. I personally know men who have been financially ruined by theft. You may know of someone whose life was taken by a thief.

There is another symptom of this national epidemic which deserves mentioning. Many thousands of people who have been apprehended for stealing are never prosecuted. It may be this happened because of what is known as plea bargaining, which means pleading guilty to a lesser crime to avoid being prosecuted for the more serious one. How many times are looters in riots prosecuted for stealing? Though people may be seen on national television breaking into a shop or store and stealing everything that can be carried away, they are seldom brought to justice. There is even a tendency to excuse them because they are "underprivileged." Because of the rejection of any absolute standard of right and wrong, including the Ten Commandments, we have developed a sociology which excuses criminal action on the basis of need, real or imaginary. Somehow I fail to see how a stolen television set meets a legitimate "need."

Now modern technology has made it possible and very tempting to commit major crimes of stealing through electronic manipulation. Usually the person committing this crime is known as a respected business man, yet this man is as guilty before God as the hoodlum in the street who holds up his victim at gun or knife point.

In spite of the extent and scope of this crime, in spite of the fact that modern society winks at many of its forms, God's law forbids and condemns all forms of stealing. It warns that ill-gotten gain does not prosper a man or nation. It teaches that true prosperity lies in obedience to God's way. It condemns all our foolish efforts to justify this sinful act. According to Scripture, God takes personal notice when we break this law. It is an offense to Him, and a sin against His nature and His ordained structure of human society. There are probably more prohibitions against stealing in God's Word than any other social sin. God is intensely concerned that we protect each other's property rights, and that we punish the violators of these rights, and that we require restitution, even up to sevenfold in some cases.

Why do people steal when everyone admits it is wrong? Why do so many feel that it's fair game to cheat large corporations and even the government out of millions and even billions of dollars each year? Why do people keep right on taking things which do not belong to them? It would be easy to respond simplistically and to say we're all thieves. There is an even deeper reason than this. There is a desire on the part of all to get more than you have, and to get it for nothing. For this reason, people both steal and gamble. Gambling always involves stealing because it is based on the idea of something for nothing. Possession of property in any form must be the result of labor's reward or love's gift. Any other method violates the command of God.

The commandment itself is very simple and very direct: "no stealing." This is the literal translation of the Hebrew. However, it is rooted in the nature of man as created in God's image. "The earth is the Lord's and the fullness thereof, the world and they that dwell therein."[1] God is the ultimate owner of all things. The cattle upon a thousand hills belong to the Lord. The whole earth and all its resources and all its people belong to God.

In creation, when God made man in His own image, He conferred upon man the right of possession and the stewardship of wealth, and built into the very fabric of creation the right to own, control, and use property. Because of this, it is a sin against God for me to take what God has entrusted to you. The book of Malachi lays the charge of stealing against God's people of old. The prophet accused them of stealing from God by withholding the tithes which belonged to Him.[2]

Man, in his relationship to God, can never claim absolute ownership of anything, but man in his relationship to man has been given this right and responsibility. It is our duty to possess, to control, and to use all our material wealth to the glory of God and for the benefit of all. This commandment, therefore, forbids that we should take from another any of his possessions unless our labor earns it or his love confers it (such as a gift or an inheritance). It also forbids that I should desire to do so. This commandment and the tenth are closely related, for coveting may and often does lead to stealing.

We are living in a time when the possibility of theft has been multiplied so many times over. These possibilities are more subtle than in other ages. Now it is possible to press just the right button and steal millions. Seldom now are goods sold in old-fashioned shops where the shopkeeper can control the situation. We are living in the era of the open supermarket where goods are laid out on counters, and because stealing is easier, temptation is greater. I read just the other day that approximately four billion dollars are lost each year in retail stores due to stealing. That is a staggering sum. Some people may steal by fudging on travel and expense accounts, or by claiming tax deductions which are not lawful. One may steal by refusing to pay honest debts, even though the ability to pay is not lacking. Honesty may not pay but it surely costs. However, failure to be honest will exact payment in personal integrity and character. The price of honesty comes high in our culture, in which strict honesty is no longer regarded as a virtue, and in which cheating and defrauding have become acceptable. Some of you find yourselves in business situations where there is great pressure to practice dishonesty for the sake of additional profit, and unless you play the game, you may be given a hard time, and you may lose your job.

In the fourth chapter of Ephesians, the apostle Paul lays down a general pattern of honest living and then becomes quite specific about stealing. He says: "Let him who stole steal no more but let him labor, performing with his own hands what is right that he may have something to share."[3] Of course, from this there are many other implications about obedience to this commandment. According to Scripture, dishonest business practices are forms of stealing.

It is surprising to discover how much of the writings of the Old Testament prophets deal with the just weight and honest scale. The dishonest use of the scale and balance is listed right along with murder, kidnapping, adultery, and other heinous sins in God's sight.

To misrepresent what you sell to another person is sinful. How many times have you sold an automobile or even a house without telling the full story? A Christian business man should be careful about his advertising. Does it speak the truth, or does it mislead others into paying for a product which is less than advertised? A banker recently told me that much of the advertising about the new individual retirement accounts (IRA) is misleading, to say the least. These are the kinds of things in our modern day which are equivalent to the dishonest scale and balance in old Jerusalem.

Also, the Bible warns against defrauding the laborer of his wages. In Deuteronomy 24, we are told that if a poor man is working for you, do not wait until another day to pay him his wages lest he go hungry and you be held responsible for his hunger by God.[4] The book of James warns that on the day of judgment the testimony of the laborer who has been denied his just wages will be held against the rich man.[5]

Of course, it is also just as possible to defraud the employer by failing to give an honest day's work for a day's just wages. Several years ago, a government employee who earned a very high salary at the expense of the taxpayers confided in me that he seldom spent as much as half his time actually working, and the others who worked with him followed the same pattern. Is this not also a form of stealing? Surely a Christian must not allow himself to follow the crowd at this point. Our conduct should be above average and above reproach for the Lord's sake, and the sake of our testimony. If believers do not set a high standard of honesty, what can we expect from the world?

One of the great truths of the Word that somehow seems to escape many who read the Bible and profess to believe and practice its teaching, is that God is intensely concerned with simple basic honesty. Christianity must mean more than attending church, Bible studies, prayer meetings, and similar activities. These things are important and very necessary to spiritual growth, but they must also lead to the practice of godliness in the world and culture in which we live. On a national level, we have pursued an economic policy that places an intolerable burden of debt upon succeeding generations. We are requiring them to pay for our greed. Is this not also stealing? I believe this is one reason why the hand of God for judgment is upon this nation, with all its economic and political ills. On a personal level, the common practice of incurring heavy personal debt beyond our ability to pay is another form of stealing.

How do we deal positively with this law? How do we rid ourselves of this sin of stealing? The first principle is that of self-examination. This is always the first step in dealing with sin and in practicing obedience to God's law. Therefore, you need to begin to ask yourself some hard and heart-searching questions. In what ways are you participating in this national sin? In what way do I practice stealing in any form? Then such sins must be confessed as such. You must go before a holy and just God and confess that you have sinned against Him by stealing from Him, and from your neighbor.

Once this has been done, the next step is to obey the Word which says, "Let him who stole, steal no more." You must cry out to yourself, "Stop, thief!" Repentance must involve ceasing to do the evil and also doing the good required by the law. In light of the law's requirement, you must cease from your sin. In light of love's demand, you must seek ways to actively and positively obey this command. This requires such things as honest work and the willingness to provide for the needy. If we were to apply Paul's formula in II Thessalonians 3:10, "work not, eat not," we might discover a dramatic decrease in stealing and a comparable increase in honest toil. The opposite of stealing is both work and the practice of honesty in all things.

Christian stewardship, Christian charity towards the poor, doing all things for the glory of God — these are God's answers to the sin of stealing. God has woven into the nature of His world the right to own, use, and protect property. We must accept that principle, respect it, and practice it.

ENDNOTES

[1] Psalm 24:1
[2] Malachi 3:8
[3] Ephesians 4:28
[4] Deuteronomy 24:15
[5] James 5:4

FOR FURTHER STUDY

1. Westminster Larger Catechism Questions and Answers 140-142.
2. When you steal another man's property, you are stealing a part of him. (True or false?)
3. Does the Bible teach private ownership?
4. What are some ways (other than outright theft) we may break this law?
5. What is taught in Malachi 3 about tithing?
6. If God owns everything, why is stealing from another person a sin?
7. In what ways may excessive indebtedness be a violation of this law?

Chapter 10

SPEAKING AND LIVING THE TRUTH

The ninth commandment forbids bearing false witness, and it requires commitment to the truth. More than we like to admit, our attitude toward this commandment is something like this: "If you lie to me, that is unforgivable, but if I lie to you, it is understandable. If I accuse you of lying, you should be ashamed, but if you accuse me of lying (even if I am guilty), it is a terrible offense." The difference between an ordinary lie and a little white lie is whether I tell it or you tell it. God sees lying as lying, and He forbids it saying, "Thou shalt not bear false witness."[1] There are many, many places in the Bible which speak of God's dislike of lying. "The Lord hates a lying tongue."[2] "He who tells lies shall not abide in my presence."[3] "All liars shall have their part in the lake of fire."[4] "Put away lying and speak the truth."[5] Some of the most dreadful words of condemnation in the Bible are words which God speaks against false prophets who speak falsehoods in the name of God.

Obedience to this command requires an aggressive and enthusiastic love for the truth, and an abhorrence of lying and other forms of falsehood. Christians all too often excuse themselves from obedience to this command, and regard it as one of the lesser requirements for godly living. Would you like to bring discord, strife, and misunderstanding among friends? Would you like to break up a marriage, ruin a home, bring down a man's career, wreck the reputation of a woman, and bring misery to young children? All you have to do to accomplish these terrible things is to bear false witness, either by outright lying or simply by failing to tell the truth. It may only require a little twisting of the truth. Yes, you can accomplish all this, but be certain that in doing so you will earn for yourself a reputation that will make a loving, trusting relationship with others an impossibility. Moreover, any professed relationship with the Lord will be a mockery. This commandment is so basic to your own character that you really do need a full understanding of this law, and a heartfelt surrender to it.

Like stealing, lying has become so deeply ingrained into our whole way of life that it is very difficult to avoid this sin. It is often difficult to even discern the difference. George Washington was quoted as saying, "I cannot tell a lie." Some of his successors could not tell the truth. Some modern politicians seem to say, "I cannot tell the difference." Most of us would agree that lying is sinful and dangerous to all concerned, but we tend to make personal exceptions. "I would never tell a lie … except to protect myself … get a better job … keep from being fired … to make a better profit … to cover another lie."

There is another problem we face as we attempt to practice obedience to this law. We are living in a time in which most people object to the idea of absolute standards of right and wrong, of truth and falsehood. The humanist contends that what's true today may not be true tomorrow. He believes what's true for you may not be true for him. This subjectivism undermines the foundation of honesty and truth. Moreover, men have discovered that the big lie can be made to sound very convincing, and can also be very profitable, so the truth is discarded in favor of a lie.

What are the requirements for obedience to this law? What does God expect of His redeemed people? If you would really understand this commandment, you must approach it positively. It is above all an injunction to speak the truth. It is not so much a warning as it is a teaching, though, of course, a warning is involved. We may break this law by guilty silence. We may simply keep quiet when God requires that we speak the truth. And we must be careful how we speak the truth. It is possible to take a part of the truth and with it speak a base lie, and this is often done. A half truth may be more dangerous than a whole lie.

This law teaches that God has given us a priceless legacy: the gift of speech. How we use this gift is very important. We must use this gift to promote the good of our neighbor by a proper use of the truth, and by refraining from false witnessing. We must protect His good name and reputation. We must stand against error and resist evil speech and malicious talebearing. If we listen to idle and hurtful gossip in silence, we have contributed to its spread and violated this law. Our use of the gift of speech should lead us to promote unity and understanding between brethren. If we are to be faithful to this command, we must speak the truth about Jesus Christ and His saving Gospel. This is the greatest truth we know and the best of all good news. To fail to share that good news is to break this law of God by neglect. Of course, this places upon us the additional duty of living our profession such that our word may have validity. Are you able to clearly speak the Gospel to another? Can you share God's way of salvation with another?

This law requires that we make promises and utter lawful vows. A man makes promises to his future wife before their wedding day, and on that day seals these promises with vows for a lifetime. When a minister talks with a pulpit committee, he makes promises to them and they to him. Then, in the formal service of ordination, these promises become vows. These things are a part of the response of obedience this law demands.

In the book of 3 John, there are two men mentioned and both these men are illustrations of faithful obedience to this law. First, there was Gaius. He was a beautiful example of how to obey the law. We know nothing of him save that which John mentions in this brief chapter. Yet what we are told of him reveals a man of sterling character. John commends him for speaking the truth. He says that all men were speaking of his truthfulness and his love. The Church could depend upon Gaius. He was charitable and reliable. He was John's partner in the spread of the Gospel. Then, the apostle speaks of Demetrius. He, too, had a character that spoke of truth and faithfulness. John extolled these men as examples for the whole church.[6]

If you are looking for a perfect pattern, there is only one to whom you may look, and that is the Lord Jesus. His life was one of truthfulness and kindness. Think of how He used words. "Thy sins be forgiven thee … rise up and walk."[7] "I will, be thou clean."[8] "Lazarus, come forth."[9] "Father, forgive them, for they know not what they do."[10] Peter's confession becomes ours when he says to Jesus, "Lord to whom shall we go? Thou hast the words of eternal life."[11] By His words, He gave help and hope. He caused light to shine in the darkness and revealed the way to the Father. At the same time, His words of truth also condemned sin and hypocrisy. In the end, it was His words of truth that led both Jews and Romans to condemn Him to death. "Yes, I am the Christ,"[12] He confessed, and with those words of truth sealed His fate. The same words of truth that meant death for Him mean life to countless millions who believe His confession and who unite with Him in this truth.

There is another side to this commandment, for it is stated in the negative, "Thou shalt not bear false witness." My stand for truth means nothing unless I also stand against the false.

What does this law forbid? The surface intention is very clear. It forbids that we bear false witness against our neighbor. Further, the intention seems to point especially to bearing false witness in a court of law. The implications are broader than this one situation of a formal court room.

The book of James has much to say about the wrong use of speech and the seriousness of it. James tells us that the tongue is tied to the heart and reveals the true condition of a man.[13] Jesus, too, said that lying comes from the heart of man. When James was speaking about this whole matter, he said the tongue was like the rudder of a ship — a small member, but guiding the whole ship, and the whole course of your life. Once again, he compared the tongue to a small spark that sets afire the forest: "So the tongue is a fire, a very world of iniquity, and is set among our members as that which defiles the whole body, and sets on fire the course of our life, and is set on fire by hell."[14] Strong words, but true. Although man may tame every wild beast, he cannot tame the tongue; it is a restless evil and full of deadly poison.

The habit of lying and misrepresentation is a natural inclination of early childhood, and only careful training and consistent discipline will correct it. Little children may be caught red-handed in stealing or some other act of disobedience and still desperately try to lie their way out of it. A wise parent will recognize this tendency in children and will not be deterred from proper discipline. The failure to do this opens the door to all manner of heartbreak and disappointment which will grow with the passing years. Parents, don't be reluctant to deal with this sin in your children. You will reap a bitter harvest otherwise. At the same time, be sure your example of honesty and truthfulness is one that they can follow safely. If it is wrong for a child to lie — and it is — then it is even more so for a parent to lie to a child. I tried to impress upon my children the importance of gaining a reputation for honesty with their parents even in the smallest things. I told them the day would come when it would be very important for their mother and me to believe their word. One day, they would want to use the family car, and go places and do things that would require a lot of trust on our part. Hopefully they got the point, and for the most part established that reputation. Sometimes, parents will excuse themselves for doing the very thing for which they will punish their children. Honesty within the family circle is the basis for mutual trust and it must be a two-way street.

This law of God forbids talebearing and idle gossip. There are so many passages in the Bible which speak of this as heinous sin and warn us against it. There is one place in the Bible that brackets gossiping with such things as witchcraft, murder, adultery, and other equally shocking sins. Gossiping is never dealt with lightly, but as one of the most serious of all sins. Yet even in Christian gatherings for prayer, Bible study, and worship, we spend much time in the spreading of idle and even malicious gossip. A godly lady once told me that she no longer attended her women's circle meeting because most of the time was taken up in the meanest sort of gossip. As a pastor, I have personally seen more grief and trouble in churches because of this one sin than from all others. Talebearing, whispering, backbiting, and spreading of strife are all forbidden by the ninth commandment.

There are many other forms of lying which seem to vie with each other to see which is the most destructive. There is the lie of carelessness in speech. I may not have known it was a lie when I passed it on, but I have an obligation to make sure. I have seen this in two forms of late, and both are detrimental to the cause of Christ. The first was an often-repeated hoax about a noted computer scientist who "proved" the account of Joshua making the sun stand still by the use of a computerized time study. The whole story was false but was repeated in print and in many sermons as "proof" the Bible is true. It brought discredit upon the good name of Jesus Christ when it was exposed as a hoax.

Another similar incident was the circulation of a petition protesting the efforts of a noted atheist to remove all religious broadcasting from radio and television. This petition was signed by millions, who later discovered to their embarrassment there was no such effort underway. The lie of carelessness can be very harmful

There is the lie of boasting, in which many of us engage constantly. There is the lie of blame shifting. Adam practiced this on Eve, and their seed have used it freely ever since the dawn of time. Lies may be told by the twisting of truth. A sea captain was once forced to record in his log the repeated misdeeds of the first mate. He recorded in his log that on such and such a date, the first mate was drunk again. Even though the mate begged him to remove the damaging word, he steadfastly refused. So the first mate recorded in his private log these words: "Today, the captain was sober." Perfectly true words, but said in such a way as to tell a base lie.

There is the lie of inference — not really coming out and repeating a lie, but simply inferring some bad thing about another person. There are the lies of vow breaking. Can any claim innocence of this? What about those vows you took when you united with the Church of Jesus Christ? Have you kept them all fully, perfectly? How many people lightly toss aside the wedding vows, often at the slightest provocation, or worse because of some lust and momentary delight. Even in marriages that are never structurally broken, the vows may be constantly broken in spirit and in deed. The husband has vowed to love his wife even as Christ loved the church, and the wife has vowed to submit herself to her husband as unto the Lord.

The most serious form of lying is that whereby we deceive ourselves. I confess with tears that I know people who have spent their lives deceiving themselves, especially about their relationship to the Lord. Jesus spoke of such people when He told of that day when many would come before Him saying, "Lord, Lord," and claiming to know and be known of Him. Of such and to such He will say, "Depart from me, I never knew you."[15] If there is a more deadly lie than self-deception, it is the insincere confession and insincere worship of God, whereby we worship God in words of hymns, by repetition of creed, and in oft repeated prayers, but not from the heart and not in truth. The Bible calls this hypocrisy. There are scriptural examples of this. The accusers of faithful Daniel professed great loyalty to the king, but only as a means to condemn that good man before the king. They told no lie, but they sought to destroy Daniel by misrepresenting the truth.[16]

There were the accusers of Jesus and the false witnesses who rose up against Him. They quoted, or rather misquoted, His words about destroying the temple and rebuilding it in three days as a means to condemn Him.[17] I think of Diotrephes, of whom John spoke. He hindered the spread of the Gospel and told lies about John. For this, he brought upon himself a terrible anathema.[18]

Why is it so important to obey this law? It speaks of your identity, whose you are and who you are. Who is the father of liars? Who is the author of truth? Obedience to this law will largely determine your relationship and influence with your fellow man, for good or ill. Your words may help, heal, and bless, or your words may hurt, kill, and destroy both you and your neighbor.

    I once heard a tragic tale of a young high school girl with a good reputation and a blameless character who was literally destroyed by the gossiping tongue. Tales which were not true were spread around the neighborhood about her and believed by many. She was so distraught that she took her own life, and left behind a note saying she would rather be dead than to live with the lies. This sin may not only destroy your neighbor and yourself, but even more your relationship with the Lord. A lying heart cannot dwell in sweet unity with the God of all truth.

ENDNOTES

1. Exodus 20:15
2. Proverbs 6:17
3. Psalm 101:7
4. Revelation 21:8
5. Ephesians 4:25
6. III John 3, 12
7. Mark 2:5-7
8. Luke 5:13
9. John 11:43
10. Luke 23:34
11. John 6:68
12. Mark 15:2
13. James 3:10-12
14. James 3:6
15. Matthew 7:23
16. Daniel 6:12-13
17. Matthew 26:61
18. III John:9

FOR FURTHER STUDY

1. Westminster Larger Catechism Questions and Answers 143-145.
2. Compare this law to the 6th commandment. In what ways would the breaking of this law involve the 6th commandment or the 8th?
3. List some of the ways this law may be broken publicly and privately.
4. Why does false doctrine break this law? (See question #7 below.)
5. Is it ever possible to tell a lie with the truth? How might this be done?
6. Is it ever permissible to lie?
7. What special responsibility do teachers and preachers of the Gospel have toward this command?

Chapter 11

THE "CATCH-ALL" COMMANDMENT

The first commandment, "Thou shalt have no other gods before me," and this last commandment, "Thou shalt not covet"[1] are very closely tied together. They deal with the same basic aspect of human nature, albeit from differing perspectives. We are warned in these words of Paul, "Flee from covetousness, which is idolatry."[2] So, in effect, the commandments end where they begin.

Have you ever attempted to analyze the present world in which we live to determine what lies behind the spirit of unrest which is truly worldwide? Why is there an uneasy feeling of disquiet that infects the whole human race? Why is there a "government in exile" of terrorism throughout the earth which threatens international chaos and brings many governments to the brink of disaster? Of course, this unrest takes many forms other than international terrorism. We in this country are in the midst of a growing epidemic of violent crime that is a personal threat to everyone. Can you not remember the day when it was perfectly safe in your hometown to walk the streets at night, to attend ball games and movies and stroll slowly home with your best girl in the late hours of the evening? Now it is scarcely safe to drive down that same street with all the doors of your car locked, even at noonday. There are many places in our larger cities that even armed police fear to go.

Why is it that in almost every neighborhood it is becoming necessary to have some form of burglar insurance on your house, a deadbolt lock, an elaborate electronic device, or at least an obnoxious dog? Why is our national economy in shambles with deficits over one hundred billion per year, our national budget completely out of control, and howling opposition to cut spending to conform to income? Why is our national debt in excess of a trillion dollars? Do you realize that if we did not add one cent to our present debt, our great grandchildren would still be paying on that debt, and their great grandchildren, too, most likely? As a matter of fact, we are adding billions upon billions to that debt every year.

Why is it that large corporations are becoming so impersonal, especially in their treatment of employees, casting aside a man or woman who has given many years of faithful service as if they were worn out machines to be replaced by another "machine"? All of these things are evidences of an all-pervasive sin of human nature, and that sin is covetousness, or greed.

In ten thousand valleys, upon countless green hilltops, in many shady groves, and in the fathomless depths of every ocean lie the bodies of the best young men of almost every generation who have been killed in mad struggles between warring nations, driven to total war by the passion to possess, or in defense against other nations infected by this madness. The sin of greed is so basic to human nature that none are free from its demanding grasp. It certainly is the prevailing spirit of our present generation, perhaps more than any other. We are in bondage to covetousness, a bondage from which we are powerless to free ourselves. The commandment remains unchanged, "Thou shalt not covet." It towers over the greed of man and the wreckage of human history. It condemns man's madness to possess, and offers a better, more noble way of life.

This last of all the commandments is unique in a sense, for it searches out the spirit of man rather than his deeds ... it does not say so much what you should or should not do, but, rather, what you should or should not be. It deals with your heart as no other commandment does. When the apostle Paul was speaking of his years before coming to Christ, he said he was basically unaware and unconvicted of his sinfulness until this commandment revealed itself to him. Then it reached out and slew him and brought him under bondage to the whole law, exposing his sinful nature and leaving him defenseless before a holy God.[3]

This commandment has rightly been labeled the "catch-all commandment," for it snares all people and spares none. It tell us that we are sinful both by nature and by choice. Even though we might claim at least a surface obedience to all the other commands, when we come to this law, we find ourselves unable to claim innocence of sinful disobedience to its requirements. This sin lies at the root of all human disobedience. Was not covetousness at the root of man's first fall? When Eve saw that the fruit of the tree in the midst of the garden was good for food, pleasant to the eye, and to be desired to make one wise, she ate of it, and gave it to Adam, and he ate.[4] She desired or coveted the fruit, and thus disobeyed God out of her covetousness. Once again, the connection between the first and last commandments becomes obvious. We are caught between the two and, in light of them both, we discover that we have broken all others as well.

What does it mean to covet? Just on the surface, in the neutral sense of the expression, to covet is to strongly desire. When that strong desire becomes misdirected, or when it becomes our master, then it becomes sinful and is under the prohibition of this commandment. This law not only forbids covetousness, but also forbids the philosophy that the end justifies the means, which is usually one of the associated sins of covetousness. Another expression of covetousness is the desire of something for nothing. We want reward without effort and this, too, is sinful. Covetousness and this deadly philosophy go hand in hand. How easily we condemn this idea, and yet, at the same time, we practice it. This is a terrible pitfall, and it brings ruin upon those who practice it.

However, there is a deeper meaning to this commandment. It forbids the worldly spirit that believes that life consists in the abundance of things one possesses. Jesus warned about this. When one came to Him insisting that He speak to his brother that he would divide the inheritance with him, Jesus said: "Beware, take heed of covetousness, for life does not consist of the abundance of things one possesses."[5] He then went on to tell the parable of the rich fool. In this story, He pointed out the danger of covetousness and what it does to the spirit and character of a man; how it distorts values and, in the end, brings ruin and judgment from God. Jesus also taught, by His rebuke of Satan's temptation, that man does not live by bread alone; he has a deeper, more urgent need — a right relationship with God.

Do you know the one thing the covetous person wants? It is a four letter word. Are you ready for this? It is m-o-r-e. That's right, more. More of anything and everything, whatever may be the object of that desire at the moment. Because this is the one thing wanted, this sin destroys peace of mind. It makes a spirit of contentment impossible, and in the end it erodes and destroys the character of the person who falls victim to this trap. The constant desire to possess more, the lack of satisfaction ... these things add up to misery of the worst sort.

An artist once attempted to portray covetousness in the face of a man. His first effort was a picture of a well-fed, overweight man sitting at a table of empty plates and dishes with a look of satisfaction on his face. The artist realized he had failed in his effort to personify covetousness, so he tried again. This time he succeeded. He painted a lean and hungry man who had obviously gorged himself and still was desperately stuffing food into his mouth and reaching for more. That is the picture of greed. That is the story of covetousness — always hungry, never content.

The covetous person never knows peace within, with others, or even with God. Judas Iscariot is a grim example of the end result of covetousness. I'm sure Judas never intended to betray the Christ, to sell him for a handful of silver. If you had asked Judas at the beginning of his three years with Christ if he would one day betray his Lord, he would have angrily denied such a base thing. He did not set out to be remembered as the most infamous man in history. Judas only wanted what he considered to be his rightful share. Just a little handful of money, just enough to take care of his need, that's all he wanted — or so he thought. But in obtaining these things, he sold himself, destroyed his relations with Christ, and in the end killed himself in an unsuccessful attempt to atone for his crime.

Do you think the rich fool of whom Jesus spoke ever considered himself to be a fool? Of course not! He knew he was well off. He had worked hard to make sure of that. He laid careful plans for the future, but there was a fatal flaw in his scheme. He had forgotten God, from whom all things had come and before whom he must now give account. God said he was a fool, for he had said in his heart, "There is no God." His life was wasted; it was only vanity and emptiness.

Covetousness has a terrible effect on your relationship with other people. It makes you envious and suspicious of others, and it causes you to hate them. It causes you to depersonalize others. You look at them as problems rather than as people. I think of Herod, the king, whose life was ruined by this sin. What began as a promising and even brilliant career was blighted and devastated because of this sin. He even became suspicious of his own sons and had them murdered, lest they should inherit his throne. His mad hatred extended to his wife, and she, too, was slain. All of Herod's power and promise came to naught because greed ruled over this ruler of men. I think of King Ahab and his coveting of Naboth's vineyard. He was so driven by his passion to possess that his mind became completely absorbed with the desire. Naboth ceased to be a person. He was an obstacle, a problem to be removed. So with the consent of Ahab, his wicked wife Jezebel had Naboth put to death, just in order that Ahab might enjoy a bunch of grapes. (He never did.)[6] I think of King David. He, too, fell to this sin. He coveted his neighbor's wife. Uriah loved David, almost to the point of worship. When he was called from the front lines to report to his king and commander, he would not so much as spend one night with his wife; rather, he lay at the door of David's palace in token of his complete dedication to his king's victory over his foes. But Uriah believed and trusted in David. Uriah was put to death because he stood between David and that which he coveted.[7] Yes, covetousness destroys your relationship with your fellow man, even best friends and family.

And what are the effects of covetousness on your relationship with the Lord? The New Testament tells us that covetousness is idolatry. Covetousness is a god, a cruel and demanding god that forgives none and requires all you have. It destroys your sense of the reality of unseen things such as God and heaven. It blinds you to the certainty of that coming day when all must appear before the judgment seat of Christ to give account of the things done in the body, whether good or bad. It tends to make you forget that a night will come when God will say of you, "This night thy soul is required of thee." If we make the end and purpose of living the acquisition of things, then what happens when life is over? What will be left? Are there pockets in a shroud? Is there room in a narrow coffin for great wealth?

I think one of the saddest sights I have ever seen in my life, a sight so sad that it brought tears to my eyes, was a picture of Howard Hughes just prior to his death. Here was the richest man in the world, according to many. Here was a man who denied himself nothing and indulged himself in everything. At the end of his life, he was less than nothing — a discarded piece of merchandise to those who had used him, just as he had used others in his lifetime. That picture of that gaunt, lonely, dying man was one of the most shocking pictures of the end result of covetousness I have ever seen.

Having seen some of the ways in which this law may be broken, the more important question remains: How may I obey this law? It takes much more than just "I will not"; it takes a resounding and enthusiastic, "I will." Recently, I was privileged to take part in the dedication service of a new building at Ridge Haven, the conference center of the Presbyterian Church in America. There were two men present, both in their eighties, but neither of these men could be called old because they had discovered the secret of successful living and a happy escape from the clutches of covetousness. Both of these men are reasonably wealthy and seem to enjoy making money, but not keeping money. Their joy is to give to the causes of Christ on earth. After the brief service of dedication, one of the men came to me with these words: "I can't tell you how wonderful it is to be allowed to make investments in something that pays spiritual dividends." He was speaking the most profound conviction of his heart. He was awed and humbled by the thought that God would actually use his material possessions for eternal purposes. Both of these men were men of great contentment, not because of what they had, but because of what they had given away. Both men are well past retirement age, but eager to put their minds and bodies to work that they might have more to give to God's work. I'm sure you would not be surprised to learn that neither wanted publicity about what they had done. They are content for the Lord to have all the glory. These men are living examples of what it means to obey, in the positive sense, the commandment of our God, "Thou shalt not covet."

In my own life, I have found only one thing which is effective in deterring and overcoming the sin of greed, and that is the faithful practice of stewardship. The more I give, the less hold the things of the world have on me. When I forget this and begin to hold on and try to obtain even more, I discover the captivity of covetousness is a powerful bondage. Once you learn to put God first in a tangible way, by tithing and bringing offerings to the Lord, the stranglehold of desire to get and keep material things is loosened and eventually broken. The joy, peace, and contentment of giving replace the captivity of covetousness. You have made your choice between God and mammon, and mammon is the loser. As you learn more of the grace of gratitude for that which God enables you to obtain and use for His glory, your spirit grows and your relationship to the Lord grows more precious and more real.

Either you will conquer the sin of covetousness, or it will conquer you. There is little room for compromise, and very little middle ground. In Psalm 24, we hear David's song, "The earth is the Lord's and the fullness thereof, the world and they that dwell therein." Once you realize this and commit yourself to that truth, covetousness as a way of life begins to surrender to the lordship of Jesus Christ, and that's what obedience to God's command is all about. It is reported that upon the death of John Calvin, the reigning pope of that era said these words: "The strength of that heretic lay in the fact that money and riches had no hold upon him. If I had fifty men like him, my kingdom would extend from sea to sea." I cannot vouch for the accuracy or truth of that quote, but I can tell you that if this could be said of the latter day sons of Calvin, the reformed churches could claim a kingdom of even greater scope.

ENDNOTES

[1] Exodus 20:17
[2] Colossians 3:5
[3] Romans 7:7-11
[4] Genesis 3:6
[5] Luke 12:15
[6] I Kings 21:1-24
[7] II Samuel 11:1-25

FOR FURTHER STUDY

1. Westminster Larger Catechism Questions and Answers 146-148.
2. Why is covetousness idolatry?
3. What are some biblical examples of obedience to this commandment?
    A. Old Testament examples
    B. New Testament examples
4. What bearing does Matthew 16:24-27 have on understanding this commandment?

Chapter 12

AN OLD TESTAMENT SUMMARY

The question from the Westminster Shorter Catechism, "What do the scriptures principally teach?" might be rephrased for our purpose, "What do the Ten Commandments principally teach?" The answer given to the real catechism question is also apropos to our rephrased question. "The scriptures (Ten Commandments) principally teach what man is to believe concerning God, and what duty God requires of man."[1] Truly, this is the message of the whole Scripture and of the Ten Commandments. Particularly in the book of Micah, there is a beautiful summary of the Ten Commandments and of all that God requires of man. I know of no words in the entire Old Testament which so beautifully and completely sum up the teachings of the Ten Commandments as do these from Micah: "He hath showed thee, O man, what is good; and what does the Lord require of thee but to do justly, and to love mercy, and to walk humbly with thy God."[2]

These are very special to me. During and after seminary days, I served a mountain mission work in the coal mining area of eastern Tennessee. These were wonderful and in many ways heartbreaking years, as I was privileged to share the joys and sorrows of a very special congregation of folk. However, there came a day when the Lord called me to another field. This one was as different from the mountain mission work as is night from day. I became the pastor of the Wee Kirk Presbyterian Church in southeast Atlanta, Georgia. The transition from the coal mines of east Tennessee to the suburbs of Atlanta constituted real culture shock for me. I will never forget my first glimpse of the small (Wee) chapel which then was used as the sanctuary of the Wee Kirk. Inscribed in the brick archway in beautiful golden letters for the congregation to see as they faced the pulpit were these words: "Do justly, love mercy, walk humbly with thy God." In a way which I could never explain to anyone, the Lord used those words and their location to assure me of His calling to that congregation.

Micah served in the waning days of Judah's might and glory. Whereas his better-known contemporary, Isaiah, spoke the word of God in the courts of kings, Micah preached on the street corners of the common man. His message was a combination of judgment and mercy, warning and hope. Judah had chosen the pathway of self-destruction. Micah rebuked the people for their sin and called upon them to sincerely repent, at the same time promising mercy for those who repented and turned aside from their sinful ways. It was Micah who foretold that the Messiah would be born in Bethlehem and through David's son according to the flesh. He would also be God incarnate in human flesh.

The context of this summary of the law is found in the form of a dialogue between Micah and his audience. The sixth chapter begins with Micah delivering God's indictment against His erring people. Then the question is raised by the people: "With what shall I come to the Lord and bow myself before the God on high? Shall I come to Him with burnt offerings, with yearling calves? Does the Lord take delight in thousands of rams, in ten thousand rivers of oil? Shall I present my firstborn for my rebellious acts, the fruit of my body for the sins of my soul?" The answer is couched in these incomparable words: "He has told you of man what is good: and what does the Lord require of you but to do justice and to love mercy, and to walk humbly with thy God."[3] This answer was not given as a way of salvation, but to remind redeemed people who were brought under the conviction of God's Word what was expected of them. This is the way to please God and to avert wrath. It was a message sorely needed by a carefree and careless generation of people, and it is equally important for a similar generation of people which seems surprised to discover that the Lord requires anything of them. This is the age of easy believism, of Christian people who speak much of the cross but are reluctant to bear it, and to whom the words of Jesus about a straight gate and a narrow way seem but idle sounds with no modern application.

    This passage gets right to the heart of the Ten Commandments. What does the Lord require of you? These words apply as much to modern man as to the generation of

Micah. It is by such conduct, as suggested here, that we become the light of the world and the salt of the earth. The beauty and power of these words, like so much of Scripture, are to be found in their utter simplicity. There is nothing dramatic or spectacular, but much that is powerful found here. Micah had no new ideas, but a simple summary of all that God ever requires of His folk. It is natural for the human mind to think in terms of the grand and glorious glass cathedrals rather than the "little brown church in the vale." So the suggestion came that God might be pleased with some spectacular display of worship ... perhaps in the form of an offering of a thousand rams or rivers of oil. If that is not enough, then the ultimate offering — child sacrifice. But no, none of these; rather, simple obedience to basic things like justice, mercy, and humility. It is hard for man to accept God's simple provision. Think of the story of Naaman the leper. When he went to Elisha with a request for healing, he was incensed that the prophet bade him bathe in the river Jordan seven times. "I thought he would at least strike his hands over the leprosy and call upon his God," protested the insulted Naaman. It was only with much persuasion that he finally accepted God's provision and found healing.[4]

    No, God is really not interested so much in the spectacular and dramatic, but He looks for those who will worship Him in spirit and in truth, and for those who will do justly, love mercy, and walk humbly before Him. It is interesting and significant that these three things God requires of us are also His three attributes which are most closely associated with our salvation: justice, mercy, and humility. The cross reveals all three in proper balance. There we see the justice of God enacted upon sinful man, when He who knew no sin became sin for us. The justice of God required the shedding of the blood of His beloved Son in our behalf. There also, God's mercy is revealed by providing that which his justice requires. It was the incredible humility of God — yes, the humility of God — that brought Him into the world in the form of the tiny baby in the crude manger in Bethlehem. The humility of God is most clearly seen when He humbled Himself and became obedient unto death, even the death on a cross.

Let us examine what God requires as it is seen in these three words. God requires that we do justice. That means sincerity in our relationship with Him rather than hypocrisy. Unless we approach God in this manner, we will never learn to practice justice or fairness with our fellow man. This means honesty and fairness with our family and neighbor. It requires that all social and business dealings be founded upon this principle. As we have seen in an earlier chapter, we are living in an age when lying in many forms has become a way of life and business. Honesty in advertising and truth in packaging laws are needed because of widespread dishonesty and the forsaking of justice in trade and commerce. God requires simple honesty by this word, justice. This would mean an honest day's work for an honest day's pay and vice versa. This would also mean that God would expect an honest tax return, even from "religious people" and religious organizations. Laboring for the Lord does not excuse one from this requirement. I once had a friend who was a used car dealer. In a business that is not always known for complete honesty and fairness, he was an honest man who earnestly tried to be just in all his dealings. On a certain day, a prominent minister in the city came in to trade cars. He was driving a late model auto with only 8,000 miles showing on the odometer. The car was almost immaculate. The mileage appeared correct, so a price was agreed upon which reflected the low mileage. Later, it was discovered there was really 28,000 miles on the car. When confronted with his dishonesty, the minister's only reaction was anger at the used car dealer. Needless to say, the cause of Christ suffered in the minds of the other men who worked in the dealership.

But, of course, preachers are not the only ones who disobey this requirement. Sometimes, they are victims of others who practice disobedience. A young minister had just moved on the field in a small community and the congregation honored him with an old-fashioned "pounding" (the practice where each one brought a "pound" of food, clothing, etc.). The wealthiest man in the congregation, who was the owner of a large department store, had the reputation of being somewhat tight-fisted. He wanted to make a show of bringing the best gift, but at the same time something that would not cost him very much. Searching through his store, he found a large bowl that gave the appearance of being very ornate and expensive but bore the price tag of $1.00. He erased the period and made the tag read $100.00. A few days later, the young minister showed up in the store with the beautiful bowl and, as the Lord would have it, there were several members of the congregation in the store at the time. The pastor explained that he and his wife had both come from very humble and poor families, and had never owned anything so expensive in their lives before. Since he had several small children in the home, he requested that he might return the bowl and take the hundred dollars in groceries. Being trapped in his own web of deceit, the poor storekeeper had no choice but to agree. That young pastor never knew till years later why he was such a hero to his congregation. Sometimes disobedience to this requirement of justice carries its own punishment with it.

    The theme of basic justice is far more prominent in the Old Testament prophets than predictive prophecy. The rich and the influential of Israel and Judah were condemned by the Lord through His prophets for failure to practice justice towards the poor. The same thing is true in the teachings of Christ, and the epistles of the New Testament constantly exhort believers to be sure they practice justice and honesty in all their dealings with each other, and with unbelievers as well.

Micah adds another requirement in his summary of the law. Not only are we to practice justice, but also to "love mercy." Here the requirements stiffen. It is not enough just to practice mercy; we must love it. That means we practice it gladly and in sincerity. It becomes an attitude and disposition. Why does God require this? Why is this an apt summary of the law? It is because God himself is merciful and shows mercy toward us; it is a part of His character, and the law reveals the character of God. We are His children and we, too, will have this quality of character, and will, like Him, practice this grace towards others. We love because God is love. We show mercy because God is merciful. If God were not merciful, heaven would be empty and hell would have a population explosion.

How are we to demonstrate this love of mercy? Let me suggest that the most appropriate location for this is in the home. It is to be seen in the way that family members treat each other. Living together within a family is a glorious experience, but it also has its moments of frustration. In fact, it would be no exaggeration to say that it may be the most difficult place in all the world to demonstrate practical Christianity. But it is also the most important place. Sympathy and compassion are the ingredients of mercy within the family circle. Forgiveness must be in the very atmosphere and air we breathe if a family is to practice obedience to this requirement of the Lord. It is so easy for husbands and wives to harbor ill will toward each other; to store up grudges and hurts. In my counseling with troubled marriages, I find this is fairly commonplace. Husbands will recite grievances against their wives for offenses which date back for many years, and wives will do the same. Such thoughts feed upon themselves, and bitterness grows with the cultivation of past disputes and arguments until real hatred is full blown. This means sin is ruling in the marriage instead of Christ. The same thing is true of parent-child relationships as well, with the same disastrous results of estrangement and bitterness. In the home where mercy is loved and practiced, all problems may be resolved and all relationships brought under the control of Christ.

  The Christian must extend the love of mercy beyond the doors of the home. Within the spiritual family, the Church, there is great need for this grace to be practiced. Our eager mercy towards our spiritual family should express itself in charity of thought and word toward fellow believers. But, more, it must seek out those in need, the sick and aged, the erring and fallen. In this way, the caring, seeking, and mercy shown when Christ came to seek and save the lost may be seen in our midst once again. So many churches are torn asunder by the refusal to obey this law of the Lord; and law it is. Jesus said, "A new commandment I give you that you love one another, just as I have loved you."[5] When a congregation of God's people will not love mercy, they will suffer for it, and their testimony will be so marred that such things as evangelism and Christian growth will be virtually non-existent. Salt will have lost its savor, and the light will be hidden.

Taking this one step further, the love of mercy must reach out beyond the walls of home and church and into the world. This would manifest itself in more fervent evangelism, more consistent care for the needy, and more obvious compassion for the lonely, sick, destitute, and aged. A Christian without a love for mercy will simply not care enough to give anything beyond lip service to these concerns.

The final requirement in Micah's summary of the law is to "walk humbly with thy God." That sounds easy. It isn't. That doesn't sound very important. It is. Jesus said "Except ye be converted and become as little children, ye shall in no wise enter the kingdom of heaven." Some people seem to think that humility is demeaning. If it is, then God has demeaned Himself by becoming man. "Let nothing be done through strife or vainglory; but in lowliness of mind let each esteem other better than themselves. Look not every man on his own things, but every man also on the things of others. Let this mind be in you, which was also in Christ Jesus: Who, being in the form of God, thought it not robbery to

be equal with God: But made himself of no reputation, and took upon Him the form of a servant, and was made in the likeness of men: And being found in fashion as a man, He humbled Himself, and became obedient unto death, even the death of the cross."[6] No, humility is not demeaning.
In fact, the promise is that "whoever humbles himself will be exalted."[7] The grace of God is revealed in the lifelong humility of our Lord Jesus Christ. He is the pattern and perfect example of obedience to God's requirement that we walk humbly before Him.

We probably underestimate the importance of this requirement in God's sight. If we would read all that the scriptures have to say about this, and how God hates the proud spirit, we might be more willing and even eager to show obedience to it. God promised to dwell with those who are of a lowly and contrite spirit. He resists the proud but gives grace to the humble. So, in this beautiful summary of the Ten Commandments we find in Micah, we see the perfect law of the Lord refined to its essence. A sincere commitment to these words and to the lifestyle taught by them will carry us a long way towards doing and being all that God requires.

ENDNOTES

[1] Westminster Shorter Catechism #3
[2] Micah 6:8
[3] Micah 6:6-8
[4] II Kings 5:1-14
[5] John 13:34
[6] Philippians 2:3-8
[7] Matthew 23:12

FOR FURTHER STUDY

1. Westminster Larger Catechism Questions and Answers 102, 149, and 153.
2. Why is this passage not given as a way of salvation?
3. Compare this passage from Micah with the book of James, chapter 2.
4. Cite some of the sayings of Jesus which teach these same truths.

Chapter 13

A NEW TESTAMENT SUMMARY

"Master, which is the great commandment,"[1] so asked the lawyer of Jesus seeking to trap Him. Jesus' answer is the classic New Testament summary of the Ten Commandments. "Thou shalt love the Lord thy God with all thy heart, and with all thy soul, and with all thy mind. This is the first and great commandment. And the second is like unto it, thou shalt love thy neighbor as thyself. On these two commandments hang all the law and the prophets."[2] Eventually, the Christian must interpret all the Old Testament in light of the New. Our task is somewhat simplified at this point by the explicit words of Jesus. There is little room for misunderstanding. According to Him, the law of God and the love of God are inseparably entwined. To obey God's law is to love God, and to love God is to obey His law.

For some, this may put a whole new light on the Ten Commandments. When you read the teaching of our Lord Jesus Christ as recorded in the gospels, this should come as no surprise. At the very end of His ministry, He gave to His gathered disciples a new commandment, that they love one another even as He had loved them. So it is really not surprising to hear Him sum up all the requirements of the law in one word — love. We are to love God fervently, sincerely, enthusiastically, and we are to love our neighbor as ourselves.

But just what did Jesus mean when He said, "Upon these two commandments hang all the law and the prophets?" How is it that obedience to the law is an expression of love? When Jesus said that loving God with all heart, mind, and soul is the first and great commandment, He did not mean to refer to the first commandment alone. He was saying that all those commands which have anything to do with our relationship to God are the prime motivation for keeping His commandments. Jesus told His disciples, "If you love me, keep my commandments."[3] He is saying the same thing in slightly different form. If you love God, you must obey Him. So when we understand and observe the first commandment, and put God first in our lives, this is an expression of love for Him. Conversely, if our love for God is to have any content and reality to it, beyond mere emotional feelings, it will express itself in obedience to this first commandment. The same thing is true of the second commandment. If we love the Lord, we will worship Him according to His Word, and if our worship is not according to His Word, it is an exercise in disobedience. It is also an expression of self-love rather than love for God. So each commandment in turn may be thought of as an expression of our love for God, and a description of how our love for Him must express itself in actions and attitudes which please Him.

When the Lord Jesus went beyond the question of the lawyer and included love for our fellow man as a part of His summary of the whole law of God, He was emphasizing a side of the law which requires our constant attention. I think also he was saying that it is impossible to separate our love for God and our neighbor. Evidently, the apostle John understood it this way, too. He said, "If a man says, 'I love God' and yet hates his brother, he is a liar; for he who loves not his brother whom he has seen, how can he love God whom he has not seen?"[4] In fact, a major theme of First John is to show that love for each other and love for God cannot be separated.

The Ten Commandments tell us how to express this love for each other. If we are truly to love our brother and our neighbor, then we must refrain from all the evils mentioned in the Ten Commandments. We will show our love for them by observing all the duties which these laws teach, and by refraining from all the evils they forbid. This puts love in the realm of the objective. It makes it more than a good friendly feeling. In fact, it might be possible to delude myself into thinking I love my neighbor, even though I stole his garden hose or fishing rod.

Years ago, there was a spectacular trial in which a church deacon was prosecuted for attempting to kill his pastor. It seems the deacon had fallen in love with the pastor's wife, and together they plotted his murder by blowing up his car. The plot failed because of the ineptness of the deacon who planted the dynamite in the car. During the course of the trial, the pastor dramatically forgave both his wife and his deacon for their effort to kill him, and pled with the judge to drop all charges against them. The erring deacon at that point draped his arms around the pastor and said, "Judge, yer honor, I really do luv this ole boy." The judge reportedly responded, "Do me a favor and don't love me."

True love for my brother-neighbor will motivate me to obey those commandments which govern my relationship with him. When Jesus was challenged by the lawyer asking, "But who is my neighbor," He told the story we know as "the good Samaritan." By this story, Jesus taught that we are not free to limit our caring compassion to those we know and like, but all men have claim on our love, and especially those in need.[5]

Much might be said at this point, and a few things must be said. It is typical of evangelicals as a group to decry the welfare state and government interference and control of so many things in our social and economic structures. Unfortunately, it is not so typical of us to offer alternatives. We cry out against abortion on demand, and rightly so, but how many Christians are willing to open their hearts and homes to unwed mothers to care for them and their babies? How many Christians are willing to involve themselves in the political process necessary to change the abortion laws? We object to government's role and abuse of such things as the food stamp program, but how many churches bother to find out who is hungry and to offer to feed them in the name and for the sake of the Lord Jesus? If our profession of love for God is sincere, we simply have no choice: we must also love our neighbor and our brother. This love best shows itself in active obedience to the Ten Commandments.

When you consider all that is involved in the words of Jesus, you begin to understand that His words go far beyond the letter of the law (though they include the letter) and are much more demanding of us than the Ten Commandments alone. If you are still confused about what it means to love God with all heart, soul, and mind, and your neighbor as yourself, there is an example which demonstrates these things. That example is the life and ministry of Jesus Christ. He is the embodiment of obedience to God's law. This is how we must live. This is the perfect pattern which guides our imperfect imitation of Him. Knowing full well that we will never live up to His example, nor ever perfectly fit the pattern of His life, we will nevertheless strive to obey the commandments after the example of Jesus Christ. And we will find in Him — in His love for us, and in our love for Him — the motivation that is otherwise missing in our lives that enables us to obey the first and great commandment, and the second which is like unto it, and thus the whole law.

ENDNOTES

[1] Matthew 22:36
[2] Matthew 22:37-40
[3] John 14:15
[4] I John 4:20
[5] Luke 10:25-37

FOR FURTHER STUDY

1. List some definite ways by which you may express your love for God and for people.
2. How does John 13 interpret this law?
3. How may we "lay down our lives for our friends?"
4. What is the place of God's law in the life of the church?

www.ingramcontent.com/pod-product-compliance
Lightning Source LLC
LaVergne TN
LVHW051605070426
835507LV00021B/2784